teach yourself

birdwatching

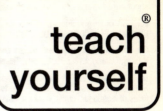

birdwatching
james sharpe

For over 60 years, more than 50 million people have learnt over 750 subjects the **teach yourself** way, with impressive results.

be where you want to be
with **teach yourself**

Thank you to James Sharpe, Nick Cottrell, Ray Cottrell and James Lees for the photographs in the plate section.

For UK order enquiries: please contact Bookpoint Ltd, 130 Milton Park, Abingdon, Oxon, OX14 4SB. Telephone: +44 (0) 1235 827720. Fax: +44 (0) 1235 400454. Lines are open 09.00–17.00, Monday to Saturday, with a 24-hour message answering service. Details about our titles and how to order are available at www.teachyourself.co.uk

For USA order enquiries: please contact McGraw-Hill Customer Services, PO Box 545, Blacklick, OH 43004-0545, USA. Telephone: 1-800-722-4726. Fax: 1-614-755-5645.

For Canada order enquiries: please contact McGraw-Hill Ryerson Ltd, 300 Water St, Whitby, Ontario, L1N 9B6, Canada. Telephone: 905 430 5000. Fax: 905 430 5020.

Long renowned as the authoritative source for self-guided learning – with more than 50 million copies sold worldwide – the **teach yourself** series includes over 500 titles in the fields of languages, crafts, hobbies, business, computing and education.

British Library Cataloguing in Publication Data: a catalogue record for this title is available from the British Library.

Library of Congress Catalog Card Number: on file.

First published in UK 2007 by Hodder Education, 338 Euston Road, London, NW1 3BH.

First published in US 2007 by The McGraw-Hill Companies, Inc.

This edition published 2007.

The **teach yourself** name is a registered trade mark of Hodder Headline.

Copyright © 2007 The Wildfowl and Wetlands Trust.

In UK: All rights reserved. Apart from any permitted use under UK copyright law, no part of this publication may be reproduced or transmitted in any form or by any means, electronic or mechanical, including photocopy, recording, or any information, storage and retrieval system, without permission in writing from the publisher or under licence from the Copyright Licensing Agency Limited. Further details of such licences (for reprographic reproduction) may be obtained from the Copyright Licensing Agency Limited, of Saffron House, 6–10 Kirby Street, London, EC1N 8TS.

In US: All rights reserved. Except as permitted under the United States Copyright Act of 1976, no part of this publication may be reproduced or distributed in any form or by any means, or stored in a database or retrieval system, without the prior written permission of the publisher.

Typeset by Transet Limited, Coventry, England.
Printed in Great Britain for Hodder Education, a division of Hodder Headline, an Hachette Livre UK Company, 338 Euston Road, London, NW1 3BH, by Cox & Wyman Ltd, Reading, Berkshire.

Every effort has been made to trace copyright for material used in this book. The author and publisher would be happy to make arrangements with any holder of copyright whom it has not been possible to trace successfully by the time of going to press.

The publisher has used its best endeavours to ensure that the URLs for external websites referred to in this book are correct and active at the time of going to press. However, the publisher and the author have no responsibility for the websites and can make no guarantee that a site will remain live or that the content will remain relevant, decent or appropriate.

Hodder Headline's policy is to use papers that are natural, renewable and recyclable products and made from wood grown in sustainable forests. The logging and manufacturing processes are expected to conform to the environmental regulations of the country of origin.

Impression number   10 9 8 7 6 5 4 3 2 1
Year   2010 2009 2008 2007

contents

	introduction	ix
01	**what is a 'birdwatcher'?**	**1**
	what is 'birdwatching'?	2
	the popularity of birdwatching	3
	why is it popular?	5
02	**special characteristics of birds**	**7**
	where did birds come from?	9
	feathers	10
	structure of a bird's skeleton	14
	structure and function of birds' bones	15
	how birds breathe	15
	teeth vs beaks	16
	eggs and nests	21
	bird migration	22
03	**how to start birdwatching**	**25**
	how do we name birds?	26
	identifying the species	29
	learning to see what you're looking at	29
	drawing birds using pictures and words	37
	enjoy making notes	41
	going outside to find birds	41
	bird songs and calls	43
	when and why do birds sing?	44
	how do they make that sound?	45
	learning the different songs and calls of birds	46
	'seeing' hidden birds	46

	using recordings as a learning aid	48
	listening to birds outdoors	49
	identifying birds from a fleeting glimpse	50
	the birds above us	51
04	**tools of the trade**	**52**
	a notebook	53
	field guides	53
	choosing a guide	54
	binoculars	56
	buying binoculars	58
	clothing	63
	telescope	64
	inside information	67
	photographing birds	68
05	**getting birds to come to you**	**69**
	wildlife gardening and birds in your garden	70
	types of artificial food	73
	siting of feeders, pests and predators	76
	natural food sources	79
	artificial shelter	80
	different materials – wood, woodcrete, ceramic, woven	87
	water	88
	birding in your own 'local patch'	89
06	**getting out and about**	**92**
	planning a field trip	93
	where to go?	93
	choosing the right clothing	97
	theft and personal security	98
	birding etiquette	99
07	**different types of birds and how to recognize them**	**101**
	an overview of some families (groups) of birds	102
	family: *Turdidae* – the Thrushes (and Chats)	102

	family: *Paridae* (and *Aegithalidae*) – the Tits, Titmice or Chickadees	105
	family: *Fringillidae* – the Finches	108
	family: *Columbidae* – the Pigeons and Doves	110
	family: *Sylviidae* – the Old World Warblers	112
	family: *Anatidae* – the Ducks, Geese and Swans (wildfowl)	115
	family: *Laridae* – the Gulls (and some of their relatives)	117
	family: Birds of prey	119
	summary	122
08	**the habitats of birds**	**123**
	farmland (lowland)	124
	woodland	128
	towns, parks and gardens (living with man)	131
	marine and coastal	134
	wetlands	138
	heathland and moorland	142
09	**travelling further and codes of behaviour**	**144**
	finding, identifying and reporting rare birds	145
	travelling further afield	146
	important guidance for birders	146
	birds and the law	148
checklist of the birds you have seen		**150**
taking it further		**155**
	nature conservation organisations specializing in the conservation of wild birds	155
	governmental and international non-governmental organisations	158
	other natural history societies and useful contacts	160
	useful suppliers	162
	further reading	162
index		**164**

introduction

Okay, so you want to learn about watching birds. You're already a birdwatcher; you almost definitely have been one since you first became aware of the world around you – probably before you could speak. Everyone watches birds, probably without even realizing it, so I don't need to teach you that!

You are one of many people whose awareness of the world around them is such that they realize there is a wealth of beauty and complexity out there and are inquisitive and curious enough to learn more.

Right now, as I'm writing this, I'm birdwatching. Without lifting my eyes from the computer I can hear Pheasants calling in the woods and the angry 'tic, tic, tic' of a Wren. When I take a break from writing and look out of the window there are a dozen Woodpigeons hungrily stripping a tree of berries; their portly forms look so heavy and as the branches sag under their weight they remind me of rotund men greedily tucking into a lavish dinner at a gentlemen's club! A flock of Redwings, down from Northern Europe to spend the winter here, dash through the sky, a couple of Blue Tits (see Plate 1) zip across from bush to bush ... how lucky we are to have such a beautiful, common bird painted blue, yellow, green, black and white. And, gently wheeling above the tree line is a Sparrowhawk, attracting a bit of lazy aggravation from the local Rooks.

Birds can be enjoyed day and night, regardless of the season and where you are. You don't have to have your binoculars, specialist kit and be setting out on a special weekend trip to enjoy birdwatching; once you get tuned in to birds you will enjoy watching them everywhere you go. As I said before, you're already doing it, and from here on you're just going to enjoy it a whole lot more. I have watched a Sparrowhawk take a nearby Starling as I sat in my car while stuck in a traffic jam. This was also witnessed by half a dozen people waiting at a bus stop just a few feet away from the birds. A Gannet (see Plate 2) slipping quietly overhead as I jogged along Brighton seafront and a Lesser Spotted Woodpecker in the garden of a local wine bar. You get the picture!

By writing this book I aim to guide those new to birdwatching to a point in their learning where they have a more resolved idea about what watching birds means to them and have the skills, tools and knowledge to continue confidently on their own. In short, it will help you find your feet. By drawing on my own experience of learning about birds, those I have taught, those who have taught me and the large number of people I have seen struggling to untangle the mass of information about birds, I aim to lead you through the process in a way that will ensure you gain some important and often overlooked skills and that you make the journey from novice to confident 'birder' as quickly and painlessly as possible.

This book will not provide you with all the information you might want to know about birds but it will help you to choose those essential books, such as field guides, and to obtain just the right one for you. It will help you to find your way around a field guide and the daunting number of species listed within. It will also guide the order in which you learn your birds as you can't learn everything at once, so it will help focus your energy where you will get the greatest benefit. I have also included some interesting bits of information that you won't get from a field guide but which I hope will further stimulate your interest and enjoyment. I have, of course, provided guidance on choosing equipment such as binoculars and telescopes and I outline the pros and cons of all the other useful bits of kit that are available. Once we have covered some basic skills and given guidance regarding any kit you might like to buy I will provide information on where to go, how to behave and what you might see there. This book is part learning guide and part reference companion. It will help you to develop the observation skills that will give you confidence and competence; and it will help you open your field guide at the right page, or near the right page anyway! It will help you find good places to go birdwatching and give some target species to look for in each type of place. After that it's up to you. I have also provided further reading and other sources of reference for each topic.

This book will do exactly what the title says; it will guide you as you teach yourself to watch birds – and not just to watch birds but to really *see* them. You need to teach yourself to become a good observer of the world around you and as such you will get more out of life. One of the best things about birdwatching is the consistent and unending opportunities for discovery. You will never reach a point where you will have seen everything and know everything but the infinite journey of learning and discovery will be profoundly satisfying.

The best bit of all is that I absolutely promise you it will be deeply enjoyable and satisfying from day one. After all you are learning about the natural world, something you are an integral part of. As the famous naturalist John Muir said, 'When one tugs at a single thing in nature, he finds it attached to the rest of the world.' We are surrounded by life and, within the animal kingdom, birds are right up at the top of the nature watching tree. They are vocal, visible, big, colourful, diverse and they fly!

This is an excellent subject for a **teach yourself** book as, in my opinion, the pleasure is to be found by making your own journey of discovery, though sharing it is enjoyable too as birdwatching with companions can bring twice the pleasure. I have and continue to gain enormous pleasure from learning about birds. I hope you will too.

01

what is a 'birdwatcher'?

In this chapter you will learn:
- about the range of activity to be enjoyed through an interest in watching birds
- who watches birds and why
- how popular birdwatching is today.

What is 'birdwatching'?

Today this means gaining pleasure from watching birds, identifying different species, observing their behaviour, enjoying their beauty, studying them, feeding and caring for them.

There are several types of birdwatcher, or maybe we are all the same. You will often hear birdwatchers being called 'birders'. Some people have a strong preference for one or other of these terms for various reasons. Personally, and many share this view, I like birder; it sounds like a more rounded interest, and as you will read later, bird 'watching' is a lot about listening, reading, drawing and thinking too. In this book I will use the two terms interchangeably.

The sorts of things birders do include:

- providing for their garden birds
- drawing and photography
- seeing as many birds as possible; this is called twitching and is usually done competitively over a set period of time, usually a year, but it could also be 24 hours (called a Bird Race) or even a lifetime
- volunteering at your local nature reserve
- participating in a bird recording scheme
- watching a local area or 'patch' to study the comings and goings of your local bird life
- making a career in science or nature conservation
- poetry and writing
- even gamekeeping or rearing captive birds.

Birds are everywhere and the opportunities for us to appreciate them in one way or another are nearly as diverse as they are.

Birdwatching in its current form is a relatively recent phenomenon, although man has been fascinated by birds and observed them for as long as we know. Birds have a powerful place in our folklore – Doves are a symbol of peace, Crows represent death and dark magic and, of course, Owls are wise.

The difference with what we describe as modern 'birdwatching' is that today we watch birds simply for pleasure; we do still hunt them, but it is not the primary reason we are interested in them. Birds still have religious and folk connotations, but our interest in their lives and the science around them is taken more seriously.

From books and articles I have read I understand that to have gone to the trouble and expense of feeding garden birds 150 years ago would have been considered slightly eccentric, whereas now this activity is at the heart of a multi-million pound industry. That birds migrate was only firmly proved in 1912; the first, proper methodical categorization of Britain's bird fauna was carried out a century or so ago; and 'birdwatching' as a term was first used in print as recently as 1901.

The popularity of birdwatching

You could argue that we are seeing the golden age of birdwatching as a popular activity. Around the end of the nineteenth century great advances in understanding bird life were undertaken by gentlemen who had access to guns (the 'sight' of the guns acted as a magnifying lens in the days before binoculars) and the means to be able to devote large amounts of time to studying birds; the vast majority of people were so busy working that they had little time to develop their interest in birds beyond what was good to eat.

Since the late 1980s birding has really taken off. People in the western world have leisure time and the money to enjoy it, we can afford fairly regular travel abroad or around our own countries via car, train or plane; lower priced binoculars are optically superb; the internet holds easily accessible information on which birds are where and this information is updated regularly. When away from our computers this information can be sent to our mobile phones or pagers and over 1 million people in the UK feel strongly enough about birds to join one of the country's leading nature conservation charities, WWT (Wildfowl and Wetlands Trust), the RSPB (Royal Society for the Protection of Birds), the BTO (British Trust for Ornithology) or one of the many local ornithological societies.

Many well-known people are keen birders: Bill Oddie is possibly Britain's best-known celebrity birder as he now presents bird and wildlife television programmes. Other famous birders include Theodore Roosevelt, Ken Clarke, Eric Morecombe, former British PM Harold Wilson and British comedian Spike Milligan. It is rumoured that First Lady Laura Bush is interested in birds. One birding connection that is rather tenuous but amusing concerns the international spy extraordinaire, playboy and superhero, James Bond. The story goes that when Bond creator Ian Fleming needed a name for his character he saw a birding book written by a 'James Bond', liked the name and used it – the rest is cinematic history Miss Moneypenny! In fact, in one film Bond actually pretends to be a birdwatcher as his cover.

It is fun to try to find celebrity birdwatchers but the serious point is that birding is a very accessible, popular activity (actually I think observing the natural world around you is more of a life skill than a hobby) which is enjoyed by millions, from all different ages and backgrounds and is rapidly growing in popularity.

The following excerpts are from the RSPB report 'Watched Like Never Before', 2006:

> *Watching birds is big business, with around 2.85 million adults going birdwatching in the UK.*
>
> *... Sticking to conservative assumptions, and taking into account comparisons with other studies, the visitor spending attracted to Mull by Sea Eagles is estimated to be £1.4–£1.6 million a year.*
>
> *... An estimated 290,000 people now visit Osprey watching sites in the UK each year. They are estimated to bring total additional expenditure of £3.5 million per year to the areas around these sites, helping to support local income and employment, and probably making Osprey the UK's top bird-tourism species.*

Birdwatching, if managed correctly can be a powerful force for good, providing economic growth for local communities while protecting, not exploiting the local wildlife and natural beauty.

And what about elsewhere in the world? The US Fish and Wildlife Service says in their report, '2001 National and State Economic Impacts of Wildlife Watching':

> *Wildlife-related recreation is one of the most popular forms of recreation in the United States. In 2001, 82 million people participated in hunting, fishing and wildlife watching. By comparison, total attendance in 2001 for all major league baseball and professional football games numbered about 89 million.*
>
> *Over 66 million people participated in some form of wildlife watching, which refers to non harvesting activities such as observing, feeding and photographing wildlife.*

... If wildlife watching were a company, its sales of $38.4 billion would rank it thirty-third in the Forbes 500 list for 2001 – placing it just ahead of Motorola and Kmart.

So, birdwatching is big business, and it is growing. This is great news for us and the birds. If we engage in bird and wildlife watching in a responsible manner it needn't have a negative impact on the plants and animals we watch. It is good for us because it helps us to feel balanced and happy and to learn about ourselves and our place in the natural world. It helps the birds and the living systems they inhabit because birders invariably collect data based on their observations. This data can be analysed and provides warning or evidence of dangerous practices such as the use of unnecessarily toxic pesticides, DDT or the effect of draining wetlands, intensifying farming or climate change.

Why is it popular?

It is difficult to pin down why birding is so popular. If you're reading this, I don't think I really need to tell you, do I? It's good for the soul, it connects us to the natural world we so easily forget we are a part of. It relaxes us and grounds us when we are worrying about bills, budgets and everyday strife. Birds inspire us and fire our imaginations from the earliest age.

Birding is possibly the most accessible form of nature watching after botany, but, sadly for plants, they don't fly. So birds win.

Case study

I found this rather lovely commentary from an American birder while trawling the internet that I think sums up many people's experiences of getting into birding. Certainly I was more interested in other areas of natural history way before I started birding, but of course we aren't all so lucky to fall in love with our birding buddies!

> I became a birder gradually and more or less by accident.
>
> Although I had always had an interest in nature and had done a little birdwatching from time to time, I didn't become a birder until I was in my mid to late thirties. A friend (now my wife) and I used to go to Huntley Meadows Park in Alexandria, VA, primarily to see the beavers and the deer. Of course as we walked around, we also noticed the

> *birds as well, some of which were pretty noticeable – great blue herons, yellow-crowned night herons eating crayfish just off the boardwalk, etc.*
>
> *After a while, the beaver and deer were pretty much the same, but there were often different birds to see. And of course there were lots of birders there to point things out, give us looks through their scopes, and share their interest. Over time, we started going more often and paying more attention to the birds. Then the inevitable happened, and we started keeping lists. That of course was the beginning of the end – we were hooked. Pretty soon, both our birding and our relationship became more serious. Within a few years we would be doing ten-day, 3,000-mile tours of Colorado, featuring lots of birding.*
>
> *We are now married and have two youngish kids. Our birding activities are significantly curtailed, but we still like to get out to the extent we can, and are hoping to expand the opportunities as the kids, who are also interested in birds, grow older. Why do we still bird? I guess the reasons we got started – the birds are still interesting, mysterious creatures that we enjoy watching. For me, a yellow-rumped warbler in fresh breeding plumage is still the most beautiful sign that spring is really here. There is also the challenge – both of finding and identifying birds. And there is often the pleasure of being out in places where we would enjoy walking or being anyway, and having an excuse to be there (not always of course, as birds are often found places we wouldn't otherwise care to go!).*

Birding is so accessible. You can spend a lot on your birding, but you can also become quite expert and gain huge experience with very little. Good, entry level binoculars can cost as little as £200 and a field guide doesn't cost much. Whether you are young or old, rich or poor, blind or with good sight you can tremendously enjoy birding.

It's a great thing to do and once started your birding will last you a life time. Once your eyes are open to the natural world around you they can never be closed. Once you start to appreciate wild birds and the plants and animals around you, you will wonder how you could possibly have not noticed them before.

02 special characteristics of birds

In this chapter you will learn:
- where birds come from
- birds' anatomy and physiology
- bird migration.

What makes a bird a bird? You probably have a fair idea of the answer; birds fly (well, most do), they lay eggs and they are covered in feathers. They are highly successful animals, occupying every part of the earth. Like humans they are warm blooded. Being able to regulate their own body temperature through their own metabolism and their warm blood (or endoithermy) combined with the insulating effects of their feathers and ability to fly means they can survive pretty much anywhere.

Animal life on our planet is actually ruled by insects, although we may think differently! Insects have diversified into over 800,000 species. Mammals by comparison come in 4,600 different shapes; there are 3,000 species of amphibians, 6,000 reptiles but at least 9,000 species of birds – possibly closer to 10,000. Flying is a winning strategy.

The range of birds we see on our planet today is extraordinary and diverse. Some birds fly, some fly underwater and a few have lost the power of flight but are still successful. At one end of the earth, species include the Penguin. The Rockhopper Penguin flies in flocks underwater at depths of 100 metres. It relies so much on its waterproof feathers that prior to moulting, once each year, it builds up fat reserves to see it through the nearly month-long fast it endures while its feathers re-grow (as it cannot go fishing during this regrowth period). At the other end of the earth are birds like the Whooper Swan (see Plate 3), weighing in at over 9 kg and capable of flying great distances through the air at altitudes over 8,000 metres.

Our planet's avian fauna includes such diversity as the urban Feral Pigeon, Wandering Albatross, Ostrich, Toucan and so many more. They include seed eaters with skulls adapted for cracking nuts, birds that can hunt in darkness with pinpoint accuracy and expert fishermen diving into the sea.

The Gannet (see Plate 2) is one such expert fisherman. When you see these birds fishing you can imagine being a contented mackerel, cruising around in a cool sunlit sea, when 3 kg of bright, white bird, wings folded into a torpedo shape, comes crashing out of the sky, the world explodes, then ends as you disappear down the Gannet's throat. Even the small and less assuming birds have fascinating stories, like the Sedge Warbler (see Plate 4), little brown birds that double their body weight before migrating across continents with hardly a stop to rest and refuel; when they arrive at their destination they will be back to normal weight. Others include the Arctic Tern, which migrates from one end of the earth to the other and back each year, or the Humming Bird, a sparkling jewel, hanging in the air as it sucks the nectar from flowers.

The variety of birds is huge but the things that are fundamental are eggs, feathers, beaks (not teeth), the unique way they breathe and their warm blood, heated from within. There is considerable adaptation in these characteristics but these tend to be in the more 'plastic' parts of their physiology – legs and beaks vary a great deal and can tell you a lot about bird's life story, feathers may also be adapted to a particular niche or type of behaviour but to a lesser extent.

Where did birds come from?

As may be expected for such a successful design, birds are no newcomers to life on earth. They have been around for a long time; we think birds had evolved the characteristics we recognize today about 150–200 million years ago. Humans and chimpanzees diversified from their common ancestor about 7–8 million years ago and the first hominid that we would recognize as human walked the earth about 2 million years ago.

It is widely accepted that birds evolved from a reptilian ancestor. Reptiles also lay eggs, there are distinct relationships between the bone structures of reptiles and birds and we think that feathers are an adaptation of a reptilian scale. How feathers actually came about is still a source of much debate among evolutionary scientists and it seems unlikely that the argument will be further resolved without the discovery of more fossil evidence.

Effectively there is a missing link in the evolution of birds. The feathers found on fossil 'birds' are too developed in evolutionary terms; the examples of feathered animals we have found as fossils are too far down the evolutionary road to yield the answers as to how and why they came about. The two sides of the argument are that either feathers came about as a more developed body scale that provided an advantage by insulating the small homoeothermic animal – from there some feathers grew larger and were adapted for flight. Or, that feathers developed as an adaptive advantage to provide short glides to an animal that ran or climbed in the tree tops – scales on the forelimbs became larger and eventually lighter and more complex allowing longer flights. When I say that feathers are a highly developed structure, just think about the difference in complexity when compared with a mammal hair. Feathers are still the most efficient lightweight insulator known to man. With all our technological advances we have been unable to come up with a material that is as light and warm as down feather. Arctic explorers, mountain climbers and astronauts all use clothing stuffed with real down.

Feathers

Feathers are the thing that above all makes a bird. Nothing else, living or extinct, has feathers. They are amazingly complex structures, we don't know how they evolved or why but they are fundamental to the success of birds for two reasons:

1 They keep birds warm. Because birds fly they need to stay fairly small and light. If you are small and light and warm blooded you have a large surface area to volume ratio and therefore lose heat easily, so you need to keep warm. Feathers are the best material known for achieving this.
2 Feathers are light and strong. They can create sculpted curves over a bird's body, lying like the tiles on a roof to provide an aerodynamic and weatherproof coat. Feathers are the main component of a bird's wing. If you think about an aircraft's wing, it is strong and light and the pilot can make subtle adjustments that result in the plane manoeuvring through the air. To date nature has not achieved this with another material; insects have a much more rigid wing which, although it can flex in flight, has not a fraction of the sensitivity of a bird's wing. Bats have the edge over insects in that skin and bone delivers an aerial mastery of sorts for the bat although it is still way short of the command birds enjoy over the aerial world. As for other flying animals on earth, compared to birds they are barely worth a mention: 'flying' squirrels have developed flaps of skin that help them make very basic glides between trees (this saves them travelling down to the ground and then climbing back up the neighbouring tree), similarly there are some flying lizards that do a similar thing. However, they are using flaps of skin, no more, and this is the limiting factor.

Try this

Find a feather (white feathers are best viewed against a dark background). Look at the structure of the feather with a magnifying glass or, even better, a microscope if you have access to one. You will see the intricate structure of the feather. The branching spikes are called barbs and barbules.

If it is a larger feather, try pulling part of it open, 'unzipping' it. Now if you comb it gently through your fingers it will mend the tear, like two pieces of Velcro being stuck back together. This is one of the things a bird is doing to care for its feathers when we see them preening with their beaks.

Feathers convey so much advantage; all birds have them and only birds have them. Other things are unique to birds, for example the way they breathe. But more on that later in this chapter. Feathers make birds and they are interesting and beautiful structures in their own right.

Feathers are adapted to perform different functions for birds. There are a variety of different types shown in Figures 1–6.

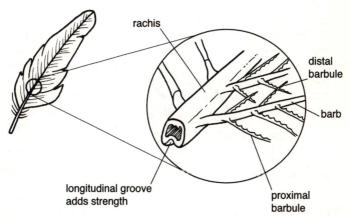

figure 1 flight feather

figure 2 contour feather

figure 3 semiplume

figure 4 down feather

skin

contour feathers overlap like roof ties

semiplume and down feathers have no hooks on barbules so stay 'woolly'

figure 5 feather layer

figure 6 filoplume feather

Moulting feathers

Feathers are made from a substance very similar to our fingernails, called chitin. Just like our fingernails, feathers wear out and need to be replaced. Fingernails just keep on growing, and wear down constantly. Modern living being what it is we don't wear our nails down as much as we have been designed to and so we have to trim them to keep them at a reasonable length. Dog owners will know that if a dog does not get walked regularly on a surface rough enough to wear down its claws you have to trim them, as othersie they just keep on growing. This wouldn't work for birds. Their feathers are mainly degraded by sunlight and the wear of rubbing against each other in flight and other daily activity. If they just kept growing all the time birds would look rather scruffy and the Blackbirds in your garden would have four foot wings they couldn't flap, and tails like peacocks! So, birds grow their feathers to a set length and shape, keep them until it's time for a change, then they drop them out and grow a new set. This is called moult and it is an important consideration for birdwatchers as it can change the appearance of birds at different ages and different times of year.

A good example of this is the Herring Gull. This bird, along with many other species, exhibits a number of immature moults; the Herring Gull has four. So, if you want to accurately identify a Herring Gull, you need to know what it looks like as:

- a first winter immature
- a second winter immature
- a third winter immature
- an adult (and possibly sub-adult too).

Birds that need to maintain the ability to fly will moult their flight feathers two at a time in matching pairs. This is especially noticeable on birds of prey and other broad-winged birds like Crows. You will see a notch in either side of the wing (in flight) where the feathers have been dropped.

Some birds also exhibit what are termed 'wear plumage'. This means that, although the bird has not undergone a moult, the appearance of the feathers has changed. They are the same feathers but the effect of wear caused by sunlight and other environmental conditions wear away the duller outer to reveal a bolder pattern by the time Spring comes.

Feathers come in a variety of different colours which make birds some of the most beautiful creatures on earth. Browns, yellows, reds and some greens are created by pigments in the feather. Others, including white, iridescent colours and the shimmering blue of the Kingfisher are created by light being refracted in the structure of the feather. With the light behind these shimmering feathers they usually appear brown; they only shine with the light bouncing off them.

Structure of a bird's skeleton

A bird's adaptation of their bone structure does not stop at the development of a beak. Their whole skeleton is highly adapted when compared with their reptilian ancestors in order to allow life the way modern birds live it. The part of our world that birds have made their own, more than anything else, is the air, and flight. To lift one's body into the sky by pushing against nothing but air itself requires a huge amount of force. A bird's wings must power down against the air so hard that the bird lifts its body up against gravity and moves forward. A 'traditional' reptilian or mammalian skeleton would simply fold up under such pressure; if we did have muscles strong enough to flap wings big enough to get us airborne we would tear ourselves apart, crush ourselves. Our skeletons have just not got the structural strength to accommodate such pressures in the chest and shoulders; our strength is invested elsewhere, in our legs and bones.

If you eat poultry, have a look at the way a chicken or turkey's skeleton is made up, especially around the breast and shoulders. Being ground-based birds, they have large leg muscles and this is reflected in their good running ability and relatively poor flying ability. But you can still see the characteristics that birds need for flight.

The breast meat of an eating bird is usually the most desirable part to eat. The breast muscle powers flight; this muscle is one of, if not the largest muscle in a bird's body, and it needs to be able to exert enough force on the wing to get the bird into the air and moving forward. But where are the big shoulder muscles to pull the wing up again? If I lift weights in the gym I employ a range of large muscles in my shoulders, but if you look at the body of your chicken there are none. The back and shoulders are just skin and bone. A bird's chest muscles both raise and pull down the wings via a pulley system of tendons.

Structure and function of birds' bones

Another characteristic feature of birds that we are less likely to be aware of is that they have pneumatic bones. I recall being told as a child that birds have 'hollow bones' but the suggestion there is that, in order to make them lightweight, birds have bones that are less dense and structured differently. To a degree this is true; I am sure that the lightness of birds' bones is important.

But that is only half the story. Birds do not just have hollow bones, air moves through the bones all the time – they are actually linked to the respiratory system! So birds have bones that breathe.

The adaptation of birds' skeletal structure is unique in the animal kingdom. But it isn't just their ability to move air through their bones that is remarkable; the whole of a bird's respiratory system is unique. The next section outlines briefly how birds breathe.

How birds breathe

When we see birds flying the most obvious characteristics to observe are those we can see; the mechanics of flight. However, it is worth knowing a little of what is happening inside the bird's body as birds have very different respiratory systems to ours and other animals.

To illustrate how efficient birds' breathing systems are consider migratory geese that sometimes fly at 30,000 feet above sea level where the air is 'thin'; simply gaining enough oxygen from the air at this altitude would be so hard for a mammal we would lose consciousness. Not only are birds able to survive in these conditions, their bodies allow them to work their muscles hard enough to stay airborne and fly at considerable speed.

Birds differ from mammals as they have relatively small lungs which are expanded and contracted by the muscles of the ribs and sternum rather than the diaphragm – in fact birds don't have a diaphragm.

As well as lungs, a bird's body is full of air sacs (see Figure 7 overleaf). Unlike our simple inhale/exhale breathing process, a bird has a four stroke breathing system as follows:

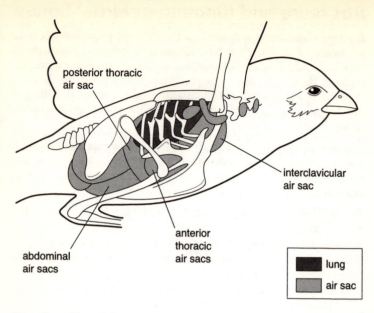

figure 7 position of air sacs

Inhale 1
Air goes into lungs and then posterior/abdominal air sacs.

Exhale 1
Air goes back into lungs and gas exchange takes place.

Inhale 2
Fresh air comes into lungs, forcing stale air from lungs into other air sacs.

Exhale 2
Anterior air sacs push stale air out.

The way birds breathe is complex, interesting and another thing that makes them unique among life on earth.

Teeth vs beaks

As I was on my evening jog recently a Mute Swan (with partner and four fluffy grey cygnets) decided I may pose a threat and launched towards me, hissing and delivering a peck to my arm. I carried on running safe in the knowledge that this was all a rather heroic paternal bluff on the swan's part and the peck would deliver little more than a scratch to my arm at worst; it actually had no effect at all. But how would I have reacted if it was a Red Fox growling angrily at me in defence of its young? The Red Fox is a much smaller animal, weighing in at about half the body mass of a Mute Swan but I would have stopped dead in my tracks and backed well away, probably taking a much longer route in order to avoid this dangerous animal.

Obviously I am simplifying the differences between these two animals a great deal but there is a reason the Mute Swan just isn't that scary. It doesn't have any teeth. Not only does it not have any teeth, it doesn't even have the muscles needed to administer a peck of any real discomfort. We all associate beaks as one of the main features that makes a bird a bird but what are beaks and why do birds have them?

Most reptiles have teeth and about 150–200 million years ago birds evolved from a reptilian lineage. So, we can assume that the evolutionary precursor to birds had teeth and they were lost at some point. Archaeopteryx is known as an early bird from fossil records and does possess a good set of teeth.

figure 0 archaeopteryx

No modern birds have proper teeth, although a few families of bird, such as the 'Sawbill' Ducks, have a serrated edge to their beak. However these are to give a better grip when grabbing slippery fish, they do not effect a bite. Birds of prey have a sharp, hooked tip to their beak but again this is designed to hook and then tear chunks of flesh from the carcass of a prey item; the muscles doing the work are in the neck and back, and the meat is pulled apart, not bitten as a mammal would do.

The problem with teeth if you're a bird is that they are heavy and most birds have lives arranged around flight where weight is a distinct disadvantage. To make matters worse, for teeth to work they need strong, heavy jaw bones to hold and lever them and strong, heavy muscles to exert the necessary pressure for teeth to perform their function.

Birds have evolved with beaks as lightweight, often highly specialized tools for feeding. But unlike mammals, or even some of their reptilian ancestors, beaks just get the food into the body, they do not bite or chew; they may split a seed, peck a chunk off a peanut or pull a chunk off an animal but in general they do little else for the digestive process. In evolutionary terms beaks are highly 'plastic', meaning they are a feature of an animal that is highly variable and changes to convey adaptive advantage related to specific environmental conditions. Observing changes in the beaks of Galapagos Finches was a key factor in Darwin developing his theory of evolution. This is because the species in question have to survive significant short-term changes in

figure 9 goldcrest

environmental conditions and the size and shape of their beaks change over just a few generations relative to their need to exploit large or small seeds.

The more extraordinary the beak of a bird is, the more likely it is to have a highly focused niche. Beaks are adapted to gather all sorts of different food and play a significant part in giving a bird its distinctive character, allowing us to identify it and come to conclusions about how it lives its life. Note the different types of beak in Figures 9–11.

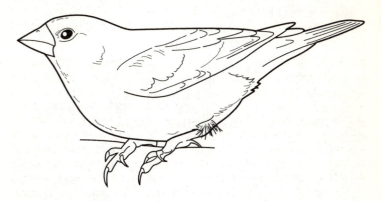

figure 10 greenfinch

figure 11 shoveller

So, birds have developed beaks as highly variable tools for acquiring food. But once the food is in the body what happens to it? How is it broken down to provide energy for life?

Food and digestion

Having lost the heavy teeth, jaw bones and muscles that go with them gives the bird an advantage for flight, but at the same time it loses the essential ability to chew and break down food. Chewing and the addition of saliva is the first part of mammalian digestion and offers significant advantages in the speed and efficiency with which we break down food. This is why if you feed bread to the ducks on your local pond or river (or even feed bread to your garden birds) you should always do so in the water or wet the bread first.

Birds have not stopped chewing all together. They just moved it to a better balanced part of their body (there is a very good reason why Formula 1 cars have mid-positioned engines – it makes the car more balanced) where it would not affect flight so much. Birds 'chew' food in their gizzard, a muscular bag situated a little way down the throat of a bird where food remains for a while to get squashed and ground around a bit before moving down to the next stages of digestion. Unsurprisingly, birds that eat hard foods that need a lot of breaking down before their energy can be extracted have big, muscular gizzards. So seed-eating finches, for example, will have well-developed gizzards and fruit-eating birds, which do not have the same requirement to physically break down their food, have very small gizzards.

For birds that eat quite complex food – like other birds or mammals – the gizzard is where the less useful parts of the prey item are separated out. Birds of prey, like all birds, have very efficient digestive systems. It just isn't worth clogging it up with bones and fur that take a lot of energy to break down with little energetic value in return so the gizzard squeezes and grinds the animal (which was either swallowed whole or in simple chunks) until all the energy-rich flesh is in the digestive system and the fur, scales and bones are left. This is what Owl pellets are; regurgitated parts of prey that are not energy rich enough to be worth digesting.

Developing forelimbs into wings may make you the envy of the ground-based creatures while you are airborne, but we have all heard the reasons why humans are one of the most successful warm-blooded animals on earth ever ... We use tools, have significant brainpower, the ability to learn, have hands and opposable thumbs so we can pick up, use and shape objects into tools. Birds can't. They have elaborate tools in the form of their adaptable beaks but they have pretty much one thing to do with their forelimbs and that is to fly. When you walk what do you do with your arms? You swing them. Our arms can counterbalance our body when moving but as birds cannot do this (their 'arms' having turned into wings) they have long necks to counterbalance the movement of their bodies. This is another reason why they cannot carry heavy teeth and jaw bones for chewing; it would set them off balance.

Eggs and nests

Eggs are not unique to birds but they are a big part of what makes a bird a bird. Egg collecting is illegal and socially unacceptable today although many excellent naturalists had their enthusiasm for birds started with childhood egg collecting. This doesn't mean you should excuse it today, but we have to acknowledge how interesting we find birds' eggs and nests along with the challenge of finding such incredibly well-hidden and camouflaged homes. One of the joys of providing good habitat for birds in our gardens is seeing the resident birds build an intricate nest and successfully rear young.

The egg is a self-contained womb. This allows a bird to produce far more young in one go than it could gestate inside its body. A female Ruddy Duck may lay a single clutch of eggs equivalent to her own body weight!

Birds' eggs come in all shapes and sizes. The smallest, from a Humming Bird species of course, is the size of a pea. Some, belonging to those birds that nest in tree holes, are plain and uncoloured; others like the eggs of the ground-nesting Grey Partridge have 17 colours. Birds nest in cavities in trees, ledges on cliffs or some, like coastal birds, such as Terns, make nothing more than a scrape on some shingle, their eggs being indistinguishable from the pebbles around them.

Bird migration

The seasonal appearance and disappearance of some birds has fascinated and puzzled man for centuries. A tale from a Cistercian priory, 750 years ago, describes a man tying a message to the leg of a migrating bird asking someone to reply and say where they found the bird. Amazingly someone replied, the answer is reported as being somewhere in Asia. Because Swallows fly low over water and roost in large numbers in reedbeds, especially just before migration when large numbers may gather together before a sea crossing; one theory was that when they disappeared in the autumn, they were hibernating underwater. A German ornithologist, J L Frisch, tried to prove or disprove this by attaching threads dyed with water-based dye to the ankles of Swallows before they left and observing the dye remaining when they returned the following spring.

Most of the information we have about bird migration comes from the use of rings, usually metal bands nowadays. This practice started in 1899 when the first metal bands were used successfully on Starlings. Today numbers of highly trained volunteers (you must undergo training and obtain a licence before you are allowed to catch and ring wild birds) ring and record thousands of birds on their migration passage and at breeding grounds.

Some nature conservation and research organizations, including the WWT, have recently employed satellite tracking apparatus to precisely track migration routes. Look at Figure 12 on page 24 for examples of migration routes. One of the WWTs most successful projects recently is 'Supergoose', which is tracking internationally important populations of Brent geese from one of our sites in Northern Ireland through Iceland, over the Greenland Icecap and up into the Arctic Tundra. You can track the project at www.wwt.org.uk.

Migration is generally about food; young birds need high-protein food and some of our most notable summer visitors live on aerial insects alone.

There are four main forms of large scale bird movement:

1 'True' migration follows well-defined routes from non-breeding areas to breeding areas. Examples of birds that come to Britain in this way include Swifts, Swallows and Martins, Reed and Sedge Warblers and Cuckoos.

2. Dispersal to and from breeding areas prior to and after the breeding season. This is the sort of movement that resident birds may undertake. Several pairs of Oystercatcher breed at the WWT Arundel Wetland Centre but move back down to the coast in the winter (the centre is situated a few miles inland from the coast in a river valley).

3. Regular non-breeding movements. Again, these are about food but the lack of it during the winter months rather than the glut of it in summer. A good example of a regular winter visitor to the UK is the Fieldfare. Irregular movements also occur when the food runs short in a bird's usual winter home. The most famous species to come into the UK on this basis is the Waxwing; large numbers of these birds will cross over from continental Europe if the berry crop they feed on is in short supply. Because many supermarket car parks are planted up with good berry-bearing trees and shrubs these exotic-looking birds often turn up in such unlikely locations.

4. The other regular movement is that of young birds away from their place of birth. This happens to a greater or lesser extent in most species and serves to maintain genetic diversity by limiting the chance of in-breeding.

One of the most attractive reasons to go 'sea watching', described in Chapter 08, is to see visible migration of seabirds. There are certain places in the world where migration routes bottleneck at a popular point for land-based birds to cross the sea. Birds of prey ride on thermals which are only produced over land, so they opt for the shortest sea crossings with the best thermals to get started from. In Europe the place to see large-scale migration of birds of prey and other large broad-winged birds is Gibraltar. If you do ever go birding abroad in Europe this is a most amazing sight and one well worth taking in if you can.

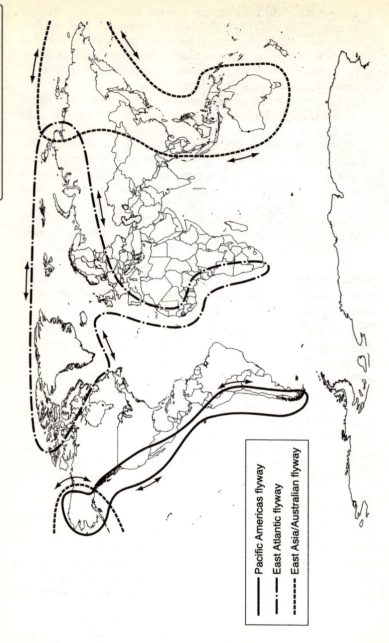

figure 12 map showing three of the many migration routes

03
how to start birdwatching

In this chapter you will learn:
- how to improve your observation skills
- what you should look for in order to identify a bird
- how to make sketches and field notes
- basic field craft
- how and why you should learn birdsong.

Why do you need to know what a bird is called? Giving it a name doesn't make it any more beautiful, or does it?

In this section we will focus on how to gather information and then make a decision about what species the bird you have seen belongs to – in short 'identifying birds'. This tends to be the main focus of a birdwatcher's efforts and skill, to start with at least. You already know a bird when you see one, you know that it is an animal that you appreciate and enjoy seeing. Simply by knowing the word 'bird' and broadly what a bird is you are able to tap into a wealth of information about birds in general, but if you have read this far you want to do more with your birding, and to do that you need to have identification skills.

Sound identification skills provide the foundation for everything else you will want to do, whether it is just finding and enjoying birds you know you have never seen before, knowing how many different birds you have in your garden or helping with some scientific survey work.

Most importantly, a name is a label, and by knowing what a particular bird is called you have a label for it that will allow you to talk to other people about it, look it up in books and on the internet and expand your knowledge and enjoyment of it. Knowing that lovely little blue and yellow thing fluttering about in the bush provides some interest and enjoyment. Knowing it is called a Blue Tit adds a little more interest. Being able to look up 'Blue Tit' and learn about it from others' observations, to record your own observations, to know what it eats, where it lives, how it goes about its family life – these things give meaning to our birdwatching.

How do we name birds?

With modern, global communication, publishing, television and the internet it is far less likely for us to have retained regional dialects and local names for things. Birds have been around a lot longer than we have been speaking and writing things down, they have been around us and we have been watching them through the whole evolution of our language. We were giving birds names way before the first authoritative field guide was published, in fact we were making up names for birds way before most people could read. These names evolved in a number of ways, most obviously based on what the bird looked like, for example 'Blackbird'; where it was found, for example,

Wood Lark; what it did, for example Flycatcher; what it sounded like, for example Chiffchaff; or where it was first recorded, for example Dartford Warbler. Some are named after people, for example Bewick's Swan, named after Thomas Bewick, the acclaimed artist and naturalist.

In the past there were some wonderful, differing names for birds. What we rather boringly now call the Little Grebe (see Plate 5), because it is little and of the Grebe family, used to be called a 'Divedopper' because of its very aquatic nature and habit of regularly disappearing under the water. Barn Owls were called 'White Hoolet' in some parts of Britain. For some reason I have yet to discover, a Cuckoo has been called a 'Welsh Ambassador', and how about a 'Parrot-billed Willy'?! This is an old Sussex name for a Puffin; a splendid old Irish name for a Snipe is 'Bog Bleater'. I could go on and on; almost every bird in Britain (and worldwide) has a variety of names that have been used in different places and at different times as the language of that area or country developed.

Of course, this would lead to problems if someone from one region wanted to speak to someone in another about the same bird. You may think that these days we all use the same, commonly accepted English names for birds but names still come in and out of fashion. People from differing generations may still use different names for a bird but having benefited from a number of widely available guides to the birds of a particular area, we tend to accept more standard, national names. However, when new field guides come out they may instigate a change. A good example of this is the wonderful big waterbirds commonly known as 'Divers' in the UK. In the US they are called 'Loons' and the recent *Collins Field Guide* refers to them as 'Loons'. This is bound to lead more people to refer to them as Loons from now on, so the name Diver will no doubt be used less. So, although we now live in a global village there are still differences between one English speaking region and another, even if the regions are more likely to be countries and continents instead of villages and counties. And then there is the more obvious problem of people who speak completely different languages! For example, a Black-tailed Godwit is called a 'Barge à queue noire' in France, this translates as 'Barge with black tail'. The French also call Waders 'Chevalier', meaning knight or horseman.

Fortunately, however, most of the people you will come into contact with will use common English names that you will recognize and differences will be quickly picked up, for example the birds that are called 'tits' in the UK are called 'chickadees' in the US.

So, what do we do about using names when we really need to be sure we are getting it right? Organizations like the WWT carry out research on birds that travel across continents and our scientists need to be able to communicate with scientists in other countries. We need one, absolutely accurate name to refer to each species to ensure there is no confusion as to which bird we are referring. Of course it's not just birds that we need to refer to this accurately – every living thing needs to be accurately categorized with a globally recognized name if we are to be able to identify, study and record it. This need led Carl Linnaeus, a Swedish botanist in the eighteenth century, to invent the binomial naming system we use today – we call this a 'scientific name'. Some people wrongly use the term 'Latin name' because many scientific names stem from Latin, but they also come from Greek and other languages. A scientific name is always made up of two words; the first refers to the Genus of the organism and the second word is its specific name. So, a Blue Tit is *Parus caeruleus* and a Great Tit is *Parus major*. They are both tits, or of the family Paridae but they are different species. If you are watching birds in North America, you may come across a Black-capped Chickadee; its scientific name *Parus atricapillus* tells you immediately that it is also a member of the Paridae.

Knowing the scientific names of things is not necessary for the vast majority of birders and you will hardly ever hear them used in the field. However, it is useful, especially when birding abroad when the local, common name may be confusing. Coming across the scientific name in journals or books allows you to be absolutely certain that you know what species is being referred to.

If you think that learning scientific names of species is too much, you will find that it is worthwhile becoming familiar with the scientific name for the families of birds as there are far fewer of them to know and they are often used more than an English common alternative. Warblers are a good example where knowing the scientific family names can be helpful in learning about them.

Identifying the species

In this section we will go through the process of gathering information about a bird and then using that information to make a decision about what species it is. I will steer you through practising good observational skills and provide guidance on how to expand your knowledge of different species, so you can gradually build up the number of birds that you are familiar with to make an accurate identification from your own knowledge, without the use of a field guide.

Many people when they are new to birding will encounter a bird they are unfamiliar with, see it, maybe look at it through their binoculars, then dive into their field guide and start flicking through the pages trying to find a match. This isn't a very good way of making an identification. If you do this you will eventually get to know your birds but it will be more frustrating, take longer and worst of all you will probably see fewer birds and spend too much time in the field with your nose buried in your field guide.

There are a few widely accepted 'good habits' in identifying birds and I'll go through these a bit further on in this chapter. First let's focus on your observation skills – don't worry about getting out there and seeing new birds for now.

> **Top tip**
> If you put a little effort into developing your observation skills now you will reap the rewards later.

Better observers see more birds, make less frustrating mistakes and are more likely to gain great pleasure from interesting personal birding experiences.

Learning to see what you're looking at

In order to practise your observation skills you will need a pen (or pencil) and paper and, of course, a subject for your observations. To practise gathering information it will help if you can see the thing you're observing really well. So, we'll stick to common species that you are already familiar with and are easy to find.

If you have a garden we'll start there; if you don't then choose either something you can see out the window or at a park or other green space nearby. The list of birds below should be found easily in any park or garden in the northern hemisphere. If you already feed the birds in your garden (see Chapter 05 for tips) we should be off to a good start as there will probably be a common species or two present all the time. If you don't, have a look at the chapter on getting birds to come to you; put up a peanut feeder or soak a few slices of bread in water and put them out in the garden somewhere you can easily watch from a comfortable, indoor position.

If you are lucky there will already be something to look at, if not you will have to wait a while and keep watching. Feeding birds is the best way to get them to come to you and if you have only just started it may take a few days for the birds in your area to find the food and start visiting your garden regularly.

Some common birds that are easy to see in parks and gardens at any time of year are:

- Robins (see Plate 6) – will feed on the ground and from flat bird tables and are otherwise tame, inquisitive and familiar to everyone.
- Blackbirds (see Plate 7) – similar feeding habits to the Robin. Males are black, females are brown.
- Blue Tits – if you have peanut feeders in the garden these will be likely birds to see there at any time.
- Greenfinchs (see Plate 8) – likely to be in attendance at a garden feeding station, especially if you feed seeds as well as peanuts.
- Pigeons – probably Wood Pigeons (see Plate 9). They can be quite nervous but, I find that somehow they know whether they are in a safe or dangerous area (in farmland they fly away before I even know they are there, at the WWT Wetland Centre where they are safe you can walk right up to them). If you are in a more urban setting there have to be Feral Pigeons.

Hopefully you will have one of these birds somewhere you can easily observe them.

Try this
Once your chosen bird is in view, write down as much as you can about it. Do this while you are actually observing the bird. You should be aiming to gather a broad range of information and you

should do this based on accurate and objective observations of your own. Don't try to do this from memory and don't look at a bird ID book. This is about your own looking skills.

You will probably gather a lot of information. Even if you only get a brief glimpse of your chosen bird before it moves away, write down everything you can straight away. Then wait and watch to see if it comes back so that you can make some more notes. Keep going until you have made as many notes as you think you can.

A common pitfall for novice birders is to spend more time flicking through field guides looking for a match rather than concentrating on observing the bird and making notes.

The following notes were based on two minutes of observation of birds at a peanut feeder about five metres from my kitchen window. I didn't use binoculars at first, I just tried to look at one particular bird to obtain some useful information to help identify it. This is what I wrote:

> *B&W stripes on back head, quite small, white cheeks, black bib, black beak.*
> *Small, perky, like B.tit (Blue tit).*
> *Greeny grey back, wings & tail.*
> *Pale underside, creamy buff. Not as bright/colourful as BT (Blue tit).*
> *Flies quickly to bushes and back.*

Then I picked up my binoculars and had a closer look. I added the following details:

> *Grey legs, pale slate grey back, hint of green.*
> *Very energetic.*

It was the first bird that I saw while I was at the kitchen window, it flew away once and I waited for it to come back. The second time it flew off I waited a few minutes and it didn't return. I jotted down the above notes while I was watching it but once it had gone I could have added some more background information:

> *On peanut feeder in garden, flew from large Bay tree with dense foliage. Garden on edge of old mixed woodland in South of England. Mid-April, warm, overcast day. No other birds present.*

I really tried to do this as if I had no prior knowledge of this bird at all. The big thing that would help me to identify it if it was unfamiliar was that I knew it was a member of the tit family. If I didn't know that particular piece of information, a good place to start would have been its small size. It's amazing how, when you start to flick through the field guide and see all those images of dozens of different birds it becomes harder to recall exactly what your bird looked like.

> **Top tip**
>
> So, an absolutely golden rule is – observe the bird as much as you can, then look at the field guide, not before.

This is what my field guide (Collins) said about my bird:

Coal Tit *Parus ater*

> L 10–11.5 cm. Breeds mainly in conifer woods, often with some taller spruces; locally also in pine or mixed forest. Resident, but along with Blue Tits is the most mobile tit in autumn, N populations in some years moving south in large numbers. Forages (for seeds, insects, spiders) much in tops of trees and in outer branches. Nests in hole, sometimes in rootpile or rock crevice.
>
> Identification – Looks like a small and almost colourless cousin of the Great Tit, with similarly black head with large white cheek patches and narrow white wing bar. Proportions are different, however, with bigger head and fuller nape which merges more into mantle. Underparts are not bright yellow but dusky, greyish buff and in addition lack black central band. Views from behind reveal best feature, an oval white patch on nape of neck. When a trifle agitated it may raise a small crest like a tiny 'spike' on hindcrown. Back blue-grey. Besides white wing-bar on tips of greater coverts, it also has a second bar in the form of a shorter 'string of beads' along median coverts. Variation: birds in Britain and in Iberia are more olive toned, not so blue on back and flanks tinged reddish brown.

There was a mass of information and subtlety I could have got down but didn't. There was also stuff that I recall seeing but I didn't write down; like the narrow white wing-bar. The main thing is that I did get a great deal of information down about my bird and enough to be sure that what I had seen was a Coal Tit – it couldn't have been anything else. If I hadn't made those notes while I was looking at it, by the time I was pondering my field guide in the evening I really would have forgotten a lot of that information.

Don't worry about the terminology in the field guide description; I'll go through that later in the chapter. The important thing is that I got those notes down straight away, from what I could see. I didn't try to write down the 'right' thing and I didn't try to get too clever about it. I just made quick simple notes from honest observations. If you compare my description with the fuller description from my field guide, you will see that I had recorded sufficient key characteristics to make a sound identification. I also learnt something by putting my own observations to the test; I actually didn't know about the colour difference in Coal Tits. You'll see that I thought my bird had a 'greeny-grey back'. I have honestly never taken the time to really look at Coal Tits. They are an easy bird to identify for me and one that I have been familiar with for years. So before doing this exercise I would have just looked and thought, 'Oh look there's a Coal Tit' and that would be it; I would have stopped looking. By taking only the briefest of notes I had a far more robust identification of my bird, a record to look back at in years to come and I learnt something by taking the time to look harder and test my observations.

If you think you already know what Blue Tits look like, could you tell me how many colours are in their plumage? What tones are the colours? What colour are a Blackbird's legs? Which is bigger, a Chaffinch or a Greenfinch? Is it possible to tell a male and female Robin apart? Is that Coal Tit a resident British bird or a visitor from continental Europe come to spend the winter in the UK?

Of course your writing doesn't have to be limited to such ineloquent phrases as, 'dark above and below, length similar to Swallow, sickle-shaped wings, short forked tail, highly aerobatic, chasing around in groups, drawn out shrilling calls'. Why not be more expressive; like in the poem Ted Hughes wrote about one of my absolute favourite birds, the Swift. I don't know if my judgement is coloured because I love Swifts so much but to me it is the most fantastic piece of writing. It embodies the character of this amazing bird. And why should our descriptions be dry? If you can write anything like Hughes, please do. Watching birds is not all about science and recording and conservation, at its best it should be about a celebration of the world we live in and of ourselves. Friends and I often go round to dinner at another friend's house and, in the summer, he is lucky enough to have the local Swifts careering around his house in their high speed flight. My friend is about as far from being a 'birdwatcher' as you could get, but when the Swifts arrive in the spring and go screaming around low above our heads we cheer.

Here is a checklist of things you could write down about a bird when you are looking at it and making your notes.

Immediate observations that you may not be able to make accurately from memory:

- How big is it? It can be helpful to make comparisons with very common birds (there may be birds next to it which you know); so a Great Spotted Woodpecker could be 'about the same size as a Blackbird', or with a common object; so if you were telling me you had seen a Goldcrest, you might say, 'it was tiny – its body was as small as a ping-pong ball!'
- What are its body proportions? How long are its legs? Is its head large relative to its body? (My example of a Blackbird and Greater Spotted Woodpecker could be qualified by saying, 'it appeared heavier built with a larger head and longer, stronger beak'). Is its beak longer than its head or shorter; if longer by how much? A good way to tell a Snipe from a Jack Snipe is to see if its beak is at least twice as long as its head; a Jack Snipe has a bill only one-and-a-half times the length of its head, so saying it 'had a long bill' would not give you enough information.
- Obviously the colours and patterns of a bird's plumage give vital clues to its identity, age, sex and race. If you can learn the different parts of a bird's plumage (shown in figure 13, page 36) you will find it much easier to accurately observe and describe the patterns you see. Again, be as precise as you can when describing colours and make comparisons with other birds you know well.
- As well as describing plumage consider the following: what colour are the legs and beak, eyes, eye ring and any other bare, unfeathered parts of the bird?
- How is it moving? Does it flick or wag its tail, does it walk along the ground with its head bobbing or does it move in short hops, frequently stopping?
- How is it interacting with other birds? Of its own species? Of other species? Is it in a large group or on its own?
- What is it doing? Behaviour can give good clues to a bird's life story.
- How does it fly? Does it fly purposefully on constantly whirring wings like a Kingfisher, or with a deep, undulating

flight, flapping on broad wings before closing them tight into a dive then flapping again, like a Woodpecker?

After the bird has gone or when you have a bit more time you should make a note of the following. DO NOT under any circumstances look at your field guide or start to make assumptions until you have finished getting down all the information you can. Try to be as accurate and objective as possible:

- What time of year is it – even what date! During migration the exact date on which you saw a bird can be of great interest. 'One Swallow does not a summer make …' One of the ways we know about climate change is that people record the first flowering of plants, first emergence of butterflies and other insects and, importantly, the first arrival and last date seen for migrant birds into a particular country. There is little point trying to work out whether you have seen a Tree Pipit or Meadow Pipit if it's winter – Tree Pipits are summer visitors to the UK!
- Where are you? What part of the world – country and region? It may sound rather obvious but you are far, far less likely to see a Ring-billed Gull in the UK than you are a Common Gull. Some people fall into the trap of spending more time getting to know the rare birds as, understandably, they want to see 'exciting' birds. This can result in erroneously identifying more common birds as similar looking rare birds.
- What habitat are you in? Many birds are specific to a habitat type, so although they may look very similar and be hard to tell apart visually, the habitat you find them in will provide a very strong clue to their identification.
- What is the weather doing, both in your immediate locality and also more generally. The weather around you may provide interesting information to explain some specific behaviour of the bird you are watching. The more general weather movements could provide an explanation of why a certain rare bird has turned up in the wrong country. A good example of this is during migration; with the prevailing wind blowing migrants off course a bird in, say, the UK may have been on its way to Northern Europe and have 'over shot' its intended destination or been blown into a detour. Birds will wait for the right conditions to undertake their migratory journeys. You may witness a 'fall' in the number of birds at migration time when the weather movements are just right and there may suddenly be ten or twenty times the number of a particular species in your locality than there should be.

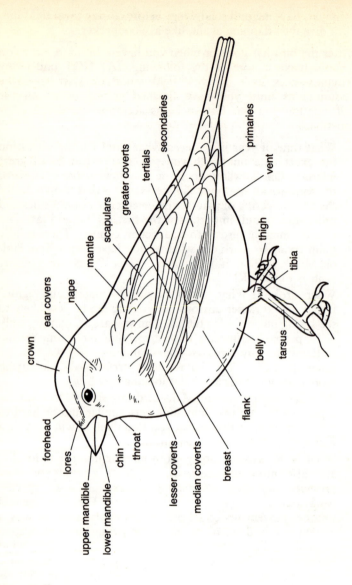

figure 13 topography of bird

Drawing birds using pictures and words

We've all heard the old saying, a picture speaks a thousand words. It can be far more efficient and accurate to make a quick field sketch of the bird you are looking at as opposed to (or ideally as well as) making written notes. Especially when it comes to form, proportions and patterning, a drawing in just monocolour can record a vast amount of important information very quickly.

The other thing about drawing is that it makes you look harder, it makes you a better observer. I have done a lot of drawing, painting and photography. Whatever your subject, I firmly believe that you will see so much more when you try to draw it, even if it is something you have looked at for hours before.

If you are new to drawing and a living wild animal like a bird seems a little daunting why not try drawing something else, like your favourite flower from the field or garden, an insect or household item. It really doesn't matter; the aim of the exercise is to improve your observation skills and to improve your draughtsmanship. So, we are not looking for masterpieces to adorn your walls – even if you don't think your drawings look

figure 14 sketches in notebook

pretty, the intention is to make you look harder and see more of your subject.

A lot of people lack confidence in their drawing abilities. Many have never really had the opportunity to practise very much and first had to draw something in a class at school where others could cast a critical eye over their work. Drawing birds is relatively easy and you don't have to show your drawings to anyone – they needn't even look good! Have a look at the page from my notebook (figure 14). With time you will undoubtedly produce some quite pleasing results and the practice you put in while getting to that level of competence will make you a much better observer of the world around you. I know a number of people, good birders, who have no interest at all in art but enjoy drawing a great deal as it is something they have got into through their birding.

Here is an easy, step-by-step guide to drawing a bird, see Figure 15, page 40:

Step 1

A bird's form can be simply broken down into a number of squashed spherical or circular shapes with some straight bits added (beaks and legs).

I find there are two good ways of starting a field sketch that help me to get the shape and proportions right. One is to draw some lines that represent the axis of the bird's body (see figure 15, as I start to draw a Blue Tit). The other is to draw a 'potato' for the bird's body and add another, smaller 'potato' or oval for the bird's head.

Step 2

It can be useful to use a mixture of the two. By getting the general body shape and head down you are more likely to end up with a correctly proportioned drawing. Pay particular attention to the relative proportions of the head and body. By setting the whole form of the bird you also ensure that your final sketch will fit on the page. This may sound like a small point but people often start a drawing by working hard on a small detail that grabs their attention, like a beak or an eye, and then find themselves having to fit the major structure of their bird around this feature, often running out of space in the process! By marking out the axis, limbs and beak of a bird first you also get some of the proportions down but it is a good way of capturing the attitude of a bird's posture or movement. I find this useful for birds that are active or in flight.

Step 3

Once you have the general shape and proportions down on your page, start to add appendages – beaks, legs and lastly details in plumage. I find it best to mark the beak and legs with a simple line and then add detail later. If you go straight into drawing a detailed outline of the beak or leg you will find it harder to get the right thickness and proportion and you may miss the chance to record the bird's general impression, size and shape at the expense of one or two details which may prove meaningless when it comes to making an identification.

Just add straight lines, look carefully at where they join the body and the angles they come out at or any subtle curves they make. I find if I sketch my guidelines for beak and legs too long it allows me to cut them down to size and get the right proportion. Where beaks curve or are thick the guideline also gives a good reference mark to build from. You can always tidy a drawing later – don't be shy about making lots of marks on the page, don't be precious about making mistakes, just draw, be uninhibited with your mark making and don't get lost in one detail. Look at the whole bird and how its body is put together. One thing that has stuck in my head from drawing classes is to 'progress the whole canvas at once'. It is very easy to get absorbed by one part of your drawing, so work hard at the discipline of recording as much of the whole as quickly as you can.

Try this

When you are practising your drawing give yourself time limits, even if you have loads of time to observe something, like a flower for example. Start with one minute, then 45 seconds, 30 seconds, 15 and five. Five seconds is really hard but you can do it and it will really hone your observation skills as it will make you look that much harder. This is such a good discipline you will find it practised in most drawing classes. It is well worth the effort.

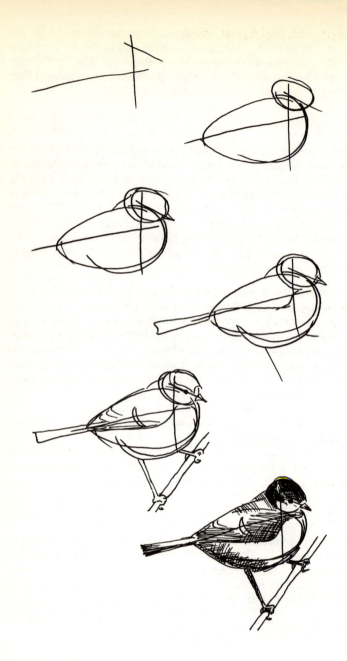

figure 15 step-by-step sketching of birds

Enjoy making notes

I strongly advocate making notes and drawings of what you see. The aim of this is to work your observation skills and also to make records that may be useful to you or others in the future. But why are you birdwatching? Certainly it is an enjoyable leisure pursuit and you therefore need to find it fun or you won't want to do it any more. One of the great pleasures of birdwatching is developing your skills and knowledge; to do this you need to put some effort in. But this should always be enjoyable. Making notes is, in my opinion, a very important thing to do but I am not for a minute suggesting that you should rigidly try to detail every bird, every movement, every detail and allow the discipline of making records get in the way of enjoying your birding. Definitely make notes when you see something new or something that you are not sure of. Go through the exercise above for any bird you think you already know – I'm sure you will find it enlightening and a good test of your observation skills. Another important reason to get to know the common and familiar birds even better is that once you do, you will have no doubt when you actually do see a rarity – you may not know what it is but you will know it is unfamiliar and that you are not just confusing a common bird in an unfamiliar plumage. But keep a good balance between the more 'worky' aspects of birding and the pleasure. Sometimes it is just nice to look and think, 'Ah, isn't that bird lovely!'

Going outside to find birds

In the last section we talked about the importance of observation skills; as the name suggests 'birdwatching' is about observing things. But if they are not right in front of you or close enough to see with your binoculars, how will you get to see them? Should you sit and wait patiently, stalk quietly through the area you suspect your target bird resides in, charge in and flush the bird or get more powerful optics as you'll never get close enough no matter how quiet you are?

This section gives you some tips on how to maximize your chances of finding birds in your chosen area. There are specific field craft tips in the section on different habitat types, so check there before visiting your chosen habitat.

As I have said in the section on observation, the more 'tuned in' you are the more you will see and the better you will see. You should try to give maximum effort in concentrating on your surroundings. Sounds obvious but it is actually quite hard. If you have ever tried meditating you will know what I mean: try concentrating on one thing, like a flower or piece of furniture, for more than a few minutes without other thoughts popping into your head. To walk through an area with total focus is much harder than it sounds and is worth practising. Walking quickly to get to the next area, chatting with friends or becoming lost in thought about all the things you have to do when you get home, how you are going to balance the bills this month or what you fancy for dinner – all of this will result in seeing fewer birds and enjoying them less, but this is what we spend so much of our lives doing. Really tune your eyes and ears into your surroundings and clear your mind of everyday thoughts. As well as helping you find birds and other wildlife it may actually be good for your soul!

So, you need to give your full attention to your surroundings. To do this it usually helps to move slowly and quietly. Hopefully you will get to go out birding with people much more experienced than yourself; this is a great way to learn. If they are good you may be quite surprised by the number of birds they see that you were totally unaware of. Their excellent observation skills, practised over many years and supplemented by knowledge of what should be where will help them to find most of the birds in an area quite quickly. This can allow them to move through an area quicker. For now, I would recommend moving quite slowly. Apart from anything else, you can put yourself off if you or your companions are rushing along, making too much noise and having to spend time looking where you are going. I used to practise walking slowly and being so careful that each footfall made no noise. Now, it allows me to concentrate on picking up any movement or noise around me and it really does help to find more wildlife. Birds are disturbed by a big animal like you moving around their locality. The slower you move, the more time you spend being still, the less you disturb them and the more likely you are to see them.

Of course, if you stay absolutely still in an area you will only see the birds that are there. You will want to move and explore other areas, so the trick is to strike the right balance. Staying still and slow means seeing more birds as you are less likely to scare them off, whereas moving around your chosen area increases the chance of finding more birds.

You could imagine that when you are moving around there is a sphere of disturbance around you that birds and other wildlife move out of. The faster and noisier you are the bigger this bubble gets, the slower and more quietly you move the smaller it becomes. If you stop and sit quietly, hiding your presence, it can disappear altogether after about 20 minutes and you see the natural world as it is without your presence as a factor.

> **Top tip**
> Find a nice bit of woodland, settle down on something comfortable like a picnic blanket and sit still and silent for an hour. The best times to do this are dawn and dusk. Dusk is more convenient as it is easier to get yourself settled before dusk (at dawn it means getting up early and settling down in your chosen location while it is still dark). After a while of being so still you blend into the background, visual animals like birds don't notice you are there and the woodland around you comes to life.

Bird songs and calls

Like much music and other pleasant sound birdsong can have powerful meaning for us and generate significant emotional responses. I was listening to an RSPB members' group chatting on a visit to the WWT Arundel Wetland Centre and one of them said, 'Did you hear the Reed Warblers singing in the reedbed? It always sounds like summer to me.' In our part of the world birdsong is usually associated with the joys of spring, lengthening days, sunshine and hope. I led a Dawn Chorus walk the other day and when I pointed out the song of the Blackbird, one of the first birds to start singing in the morning, a gentleman who was relatively new to birdwatching described it as, 'one of those sounds that makes you glad to be alive'.

Sometimes you can't see birds or, more likely, the sound they make is your first clue to their presence. Many birds are easier to identify by song or call than visually. In certain habitats and at certain times of year you have far less chance of seeing the bird than you do hearing it, for example in woodland.

To work out how many individual birds of different species are breeding in a particular area, we count singing males. If a male is singing regularly in the same place over a period of time we know he has established a territory. We can then assume that breeding is taking place. To find and record each nest in an area would be extremely difficult, disruptive to the birds and other wildlife and involve an awful lot of tree climbing and dragging oneself through hedges!

If you want to participate in breeding bird censuses, or to just enjoy knowing how many birds are breeding in your local patch or garden, song is the way to do it. I really enjoy knowing that certain individuals of different species are breeding in my area and how many of them. I can make notes or remember where birds breed each year and see if they are back there the following year.

If you join the British Trust for Ornithology's (BTO) breeding birds' survey they will send you a free CD or tape of common songs and calls of British birds.

When and why do birds sing?

Bird song is about attracting a mate and establishing territory. For example, a male Blue Tit has an average life expectancy of three years, and will be one year old when he is first able to breed. In order to breed he will need to compete with other males for territory and the attentions of the best females; he may not get another chance. He may be able to impress with visual displays alone, but sound, namely song, carries further and may be a more impressive signal.

The lengthening days and increased food availability during spring encourage birds to breed. As birdsong is about attracting a mate, birds in the northern hemisphere tend to sing during the early spring; depending on the species they will gradually sing less as they become more successfully occupied with parenthood or even as soon as they have found a mate (as is the case for the Pied Flycatcher; the male ceases song as soon as he is successfully paired up). In other parts of the world where the climate is stable and dry, and day length is constant, rainfall may trigger reproductive behaviour and therefore birdsong.

Birds make a variety of other sounds throughout the year, commonly because they are anxious ('alarm' calls) or just appear to want to stay in touch with others around them ('contact' calls). Some of these calls are easy to learn, others are a little trickier than song to pin down to a specific species. This is by design as sometimes birds will benefit from a communication that is understood by a species other than its own. For example, if a Sparrowhawk is patrolling the area, Great Tits will benefit from understanding the Dunnock's alarm call in response to finding itself in this situation. What we refer to as bird 'song' has a sexual and territorial element and so tends to be quite specific to each species – it wouldn't be of much use for a female Spotted Flycatcher to be attracted to the song of a Blackbird!

The birds that have the greatest vocal ability tend to be the group we call Passerines; these are perching birds which include thrushes, tits and warblers.

How do they make that sound?

Apart from humans, birds are the most vocal of all animals. So how do they make all those wonderful sounds that can include the most extraordinary mimicry and bursts of song lasting many minutes or even hours?

Birds create sound in a different way to us, although the principle is basically the same – air passes over vocal chords to create vibrations. They do have tongues but do not possess the ability to manipulate sound with a muscular, fleshy mouth. Birds produce sound with an organ called the syrinx. This is located deeper in the body of a bird and has two passages running through it, enabling the bird to continue singing and breathing at the same time.

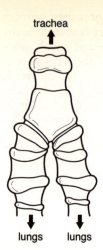

figure 16 diagram of syrinx

Learning the different songs and calls of birds

The best way to learn the songs and calls of birds is to go outside with your binoculars, give yourself plenty of time and when you hear a bird singing or calling, try to gain a clear view of it.

Once I have watched a bird while it is singing or calling it makes a connection in my head. This is far harder to achieve than by trying to learn from recordings alone. As with all birdwatching, there is no substitute for actually getting out there and doing it for real.

'Seeing' hidden birds

The closest thing to being able to see round corners and through bushes to find birds that are too well hidden to be seen is to learn to use your ears. Two things necessary in order to enjoy birding more are to learn to recognize the songs and calls of birds and to make notes.

Sound travels round corners, through trees and bushes and often conveys more precise information than eyes can over even quite small distances. There are a number of species of bird that look very similar and are hard to tell apart in the field but their calls are very distinctive and totally different.

Good fieldcraft and good birding must involve good use of your ears. Birding is so much about what you hear rather than what you see. A Birder's Club for the blind could find as many birds (if not more) and enjoy birding as much as a group of birders with full sight. There is an 'Outta sight birding Tournament' in the USA, where blind contestants compete in the traditional 'Bird Race' – the aim being to find more birds than the other people or teams – except they do this purely by sound. Fully sighted contestants can enter although they have to be blindfolded.

Between 70 and 80 per cent of birds can be found by using ears first and eyes second. One of the mistakes I made when I started getting interested in watching wild birds was to spend a lot of time going through my field guide, watching birds in the wild and learning about how they looked, without balancing this with learning how they sound. At the time I thought that learning birdsongs and calls was something for 'advanced' birders and left it till later in my learning. My advice now? Learn songs and calls at the earliest stage; if you want to learn what a bird looks like, where it lives and what it does then learn how it sounds at the same time. I promise you'll be glad you did.

If you are unfamiliar with your singing bird you should take notes on its visual appearance (as described earlier in the chapter) as well as trying to describe the sound it is making. If you can start with common birds you may already recognize them visually. If this is the case take time to really get to know the sounds they make – don't just hear it once and 'tick it off'.

Common birds are exactly that: common. So the more common and familiar birds will give you lots of opportunity to get to know them well. Don't pass up on this opportunity in your desire to learn lots of different species. A little discipline early on will pay off in the future. Don't worry about trying to find anything rare at this stage; the more familiar you are with the everyday species you encounter the more likely you will be to pick up something unusual. I know the songs and calls of all the birds in my area, but there are plenty of bird species that I am not familiar with; this doesn't really matter to me as when I hear something unusual I might not know it terribly well but what I do know is that it *is* unusual. If you get to know the song of, say, the Reed Warbler 100 per cent you will know when you hear a rarer but similar warbler in your local reedbed. If you try to learn everything, including the rarities, and only get 40 per cent familiar with all of them I think you are much more likely to be uncertain of what you are hearing.

Pay special attention to learning the calls of the following groups of birds:

- woodland birds (which include many of our garden/parkland birds because they are mainly birds of woodland edge)
- heathland and moorland birds
- birds of prey
- shorebirds, especially waders
- farmland birds.

Using recordings as a learning aid

Of course going out into the field for hours, finding birds and trying to observe them singing or calling is hard work and it is time consuming. Fortunately, we can listen to and learn birdsong whenever and wherever we want, whether on CD, tape, video, MP3, DVD Rom, CD Rom or downloaded from the internet.

At first learning birdsong is not easy but ultimately provides great satisfaction; many people find it is just a mass of twitters and churrs to start with. We seem to be naturally inclined to access the world visually but the time spent learning the sounds of birds will be worth it, even though it will frustrate you more than any other aspect of learning about birds. If you are already musically inclined you may of course find it easier.

As with learning birdsong in the field, start with the more common species. Take the time to listen to recordings of birds you already know, as there may be certain vocalizations that you haven't heard even the most common bird make yet. There is a commonly quoted rule to UK birding; if you are in woodland-type habitat and you hear something unusual, it is probably a Great Tit – one of the most common birds around, which employs such a wide range of vocalizations and mimicry, that even experienced birders are often wrongfooted.

If you have an MP3 player, iPod, handheld computer or mobile phone you may like to put together 'playlists' of the birds you think you may hear or are trying to learn. Recorded CDs or other media list birdsong usually in taxonomic order, so the birds are categorized in terms of their evolutionary links and history. This may not be the way you want to listen to them when getting to know them. Sometimes birds from quite different families sound similar to the beginner and it may be really helpful to put lists together so that you can hear the recordings next to each other and sort out the differences.

It can also be helpful to download recordings of the birds you know you will hear and leave the others at home, to make it easier to scroll through the recordings you have. One way I do this is by setting up playlists of birds from particular habitat types, as you are more likely to see them this way in the field. Having the ability to hear the recording on headphones while you are listening to the bird in the field can be really useful in confirming whether or not you have got it right. Birds often sound different in the field than they do on even the best recordings. There are a few species that I have no problem with identifying from recordings but in the field, with maybe a different quality of sound and background noise, it can be much more challenging.

Of course, if you have access to recordings of birds you can learn birds that may be common in other areas but not your own. For example, if you were planning a visit to some heathland, as well as preparing by looking up the common birds in your field guide, you can also practise learning and recognising their sounds before you even set foot in the heathland.

Listening to birds outdoors

Spring is the time for birdsong and you should try to get up before dawn at least once to go out to some woodland and hear the dawn chorus, it is one of the most inspiring, uplifting things in nature. But if you are new to birdsong and try to identify birds in this context, with a different bird singing from every tree, you may find it very hard to isolate the sound of one bird against the wall of sound behind it.

Maybe start listening early in the year. Thrushes sing from mid-January in the UK and they are an important songster to get to know. Gradually more resident species will start to sing as the spring advances until April when all the migrants come flooding in and it can then feel overwhelming. You could try just choosing a few of the most common spring migrants and going out to find them, or maybe songsters from different habitats. In late summer birds will sing again but unlike the spring there will only be a few individuals singing. These birds will include spring/summer migrants that you may have missed at the start of the season, so you may have another chance to hear them and practise recognizing their songs and calls. At the beginning of August, at the WWT Arundel Wetland Centre, Reed Warblers and Reed Buntings are singing from the reeds, with the occasional Willow Warbler and Chiffchaff as well as a good number of the resident birds that are here all year round.

Another tip for isolating a specific bird from background noise is to cup your hands behind your ears. Your ears are placed on the side of your head and hear in 360 degrees. This is great as your ears are 'looking' all round you for birds while your eyes only look where your face is pointing. But when it comes to pinpointing the direction of a sound our side-mounted ears are only so good. Owls hunt largely using sound; the shape of the feathering around their satellite-dish face channels the sound and helps to assess its direction. Cupping your hands behind your ears achieves the same thing and also can enhance the quality of the particular song you are trying to hear. If you still have trouble sorting out where the singing bird is, try moving your head slightly from side to side, still with your hands cupped behind your ears, a bit like a radar dish scanning at an airport or on a ship.

So, to summarize. Learn birdsongs and calls, start with common resident birds that you have a good chance of hearing through the full length of the spring/summer season. Learn one at a time really well and you will soon have picked up an impressive number if you persevere.

Identifying birds from a fleeting glimpse

Sometimes you just don't have time to observe a bird thoroughly, take notes and hear it sing or call. Just a flash of tail into a bush and it has gone.

You will often be able to carefully pursue your mystery bird; you might even find it was the advance party of a flock and before you know it there will be dozens of its kind all around you. But when all you get is a glimpse and you can't find any more, what do you do?

Do not fall into the trap of identifying every bird. Even an expert will not manage this. You will not be a good birdwatcher if you make wild identifications of poorly seen birds.

Make sure you try the following:

- Get to know the key identification features of the most common species from your field guide.
- Spend lots of time watching common species in your garden and local patch.
- When you see a bird fleetingly, just focus on its 'jizz' (general impression, size and shape) and any distinguishing features. Bear in mind the rule that if a bird is common in a particular habitat and your bird appears to resemble it, it probably is that common bird.

The birds above us

Identifying birds in flight can be difficult. You generally have much less information to go on and there are a number of pitfalls to consider when making an identification.

Markings and colours can be hard to see from a distance and against a bright sky. Birds will hold their wings in all sorts of ways, not necessarily the characteristic shape your field guide describes and it can be hard to judge size when something is so far away and there is nothing near to it for reference.

Get to know the more common species as well as you can in flight and you will have a sound reference with which to compare other birds. Pay particular attention to the way birds move in the air – the way a large bird flaps its wings can be a better indicator of its size than how big it appears. Style of flight can be very helpful and if you are watching a bird in a bright sky wait until it goes across a patch of blue or a dark cloud as this can give you a better look at any markings as the bird's colours will not be 'burnt out' as they are when against a bright background.

In this chapter you will learn:
- what equipment you will need for successful birdwatching
- what to look for when choosing a field guide
- how to choose and use binoculars and telescopes
- tips on what to wear
- what more advanced equipment is available for other aspects of birding.

A notebook

This is possibly the most underrated but arguably the most important bit of kit you can take with you when birdwatching. Sadly its use appears to be declining. Recent innovations allow us to take high quality, digital images through our telescopes relatively quickly and easily; this is called 'digiscoping', more on this later in the chapter. In the past taking an equivalent image would be possible only with thousands of pounds' worth of camera equipment and hours or days spent getting a hide set up close enough to your target bird for a good frame-filling image. The camera isn't 'dead' however, as digiscoped images are not up to the same quality, but they are good and a digiscoped snap can provide the visual information that you realistically could have recorded only with a sketch in the past.

There is nothing wrong with a digiscoped image, if you can afford it. However, when you are starting out birdwatching, having to look hard enough to make a reasonably accurate sketch forces you to look closer than you would otherwise. In this regard making sketches is an essential practice in training yourself to be a better observer and getting to know the details of a bird's body and proportions.

A good notebook for the field should be hardback as it is going to get a lot of use and abuse. A soft-covered book will be in tatters after hours in your hand and pocket. It should be large enough to take decent notes on comfortably but small enough to fit easily into your bag or large pocket. I use an A5, ring bound hardback. Being ring bound means it folds open flat or all the way round. It isn't as robust as a hardback book with a spine but it is much easier to write in. If you can get a notebook with blank and lined pages on opposite sides this would be ideal, otherwise a blank page gives you more flexibility.

At the end of the day we are all different, one of the things that makes notebooks so special is that they are personal, so find something that works for you but do make notes – even if you use old paper napkins!

Field guides

A good field guide is one of your essential pieces of kit. You can look at birds, you can record what you see but at some point you are going to need some reference that goes beyond your current knowledge if you are going to learn about birds and be able to identify them successfully.

The primary function of a field guide is to provide you with a reference by which you will be able to make decisions about the species of birds you are seeing, find out their name, some basic information about their life story and therefore be able to further your enjoyment and study of the birds you see.

Field guides are good for other things too. As well as helping you to identify and learn about the birds you have seen they also provide a window into the huge variety of birds – some common but possibly only in a different habitat or region from your own, and some rare or foreign. They allow you to dream about birds you have never seen but would love to see and they provide a very valuable learning aid for time when you are not actually watching birds. Spending evenings flicking through a well-illustrated field guide is an enjoyable aspect of birdwatching. Perhaps you will be motivated to plan a trip further away in order to see a bird that has particularly caught your interest or maybe you will just hone your knowledge of what is in your own back yard. Your field guide(s) will provide the basis for your 'homework' as well as your fieldwork. For this reason I would suggest you get a book to start with, as opposed to a digital guide. The various CD/DVD-Roms and other multi-media materials are excellent but at the time of writing the easiest reference material to navigate is still a book – you just flick the pages. Don't be frightened to scrawl notes in your field guide. The easiest ways of identifying birds are often subtle and personal and may not be covered in the guide. Many people have a mint copy for armchair use and a scruffy, falling-to-bits copy for the field.

Choosing a guide

The first thing to consider is the range a guide will cover. If you are planning to go birding in your own country or region it goes without saying that the guide should cover this area. But how much more? The huge range of different bird species can be daunting as well as exciting to the novice birder, so you may want to start with a guide that covers just the birds that regularly appear in your country, rather than one that comprehensively lists every bird in your continent, including occasional migrants from elsewhere and rare vagrants from the other side of the Atlantic, for example.

My first guide covered British birds only and listed less than 250 species, concentrating on those birds that appeared regularly in Britain. I still enjoy looking at it now but it is of little practical use as a field guide. It is more of a coffee table book, being quite large and with beautiful big illustrations. From a practical point of view it is too large, out of date, does not cover a comprehensive enough range of species and does not provide enough information on the birds it does cover. But my needs are different now and it did the job when I first was given it. It was simple enough not to be daunting and the illustrations inspired me to go to see the birds in real life. In short, it developed my interest.

My current guide covers not just Britain but Europe, most of the Middle East and North Africa. It lists 722 species, nearly three times as many as my first guide. But it is right for me now, in fact sometimes it is frustrating that it does not supply enough information. I also have whole books dedicated to just one group of birds, or even one species or habitat. Your first books (and other multi-media guides) should be right for you, they will help you to nurture your interest and it will grow. You will want to dig deeper, learn more, perhaps find a special area of interest and dig deeper still. The point is, you should go for what you find engaging, not necessarily a guide that is 'the best', most comprehensive, biggest, etc.

Some key points when choosing your field guide

Avoid second-hand bookshops. Old bird books are fascinating and part of their appeal is that they are out of date. For example, my first bird book listed Little Egrets as a rarity in Britain. They are to be found along most of our coastline these days and can be classed as a common species. Whether it is down to climate change or just the natural ebb and flow of species distribution as they gain competitive advantage or lose it, the status and distribution of birds is changing all the time and significant changes happen quite fast.

Avoid photo guides to start with. They can be interesting and useful as a second point of reference but photographers have a far more constrained process in making their images than illustrators do. The quality of the visual information in a modern illustrated field guide is hugely impressive. Illustrators will have gathered a large amount of information about the bird and will aim to present the illustration in such a way as to provide you with the most useful image of the bird. A photographer is constrained by actually having to take 'that picture'. An illustrator just needs to make it from the mind's eye, carefully referenced against a range of factual information.

It is useful to have a range of illustrations for each species but not absolutely necessary. Multi-media guides are useful; as well as illustrations you will get to see moving images of birds in flight, singing and performing other characteristic movements. Key things to look for are different plumages (breeding plumage/winter plumage and juvenile plumages), birds in flight as well as on the ground and any other diagnostic displays or other behaviour. But most of all, you should enjoy the images. If you enjoy looking at the images you are more likely to look at them. If you look at them you will learn, worry about the detail later.

Other essential information:

- status (is it rare, common or rare but increasing in numbers?)
- resident or migrant
- distribution (is it a northern species or southern, is it localized or widespread? This may relate to the next point)
- habitat (few birds are generalists, so knowing the preferred habitat of a bird is vital in both finding it and often in correctly identifying it too)
- voice (recordings are the main reference for this but if you are buying a book, the written description of a bird's voice can be a very useful tool for learning and identification)
- key behaviour (is it solitary or gregarious? Does it eat other animals or does it eat plants?)
- jizz – general impression, size and shape.

Binoculars

Binoculars are considered to be essential kit for watching birds in this day and age. Some very famous birders spent years in their youth watching birds with nothing more than their bare eyes, and when we first started to approach the identification of birds with some degree of scientific rigour, the sight of a gun made the birds come closer rather than the magnifying properties of a lens but these days are long past. So, if you are going to enjoy your birdwatching you really do need to get yourself the best pair of binoculars you can afford. Even if your main interest is watching birds in your garden where you can attract them closer with feeding stations and artificial nesting boxes, you will still get great benefit from the visual performance of modern optics.

A telescope can wait, but binoculars are an essential bit of kit. Fortunately, the quality of modern binoculars is so good that even those at the bottom of the price range are excellent and will add tremendous value to your birding experience. Good binoculars for birding cost between £200 and £1,000 in the UK and every model from a good manufacturer presents excellent value for money. The key is getting those that are right for you.

I bought the best pair of binoculars I could afford about ten years ago, a lower to mid-priced pair that felt right for me. I didn't know they were going to last me that long when I bought them. I was thrilled with them then and still am every time I pick them up now. If I could calculate the number of hours, days and weeks they have been round my neck, the cost per hour of bird and wildlife watching could barely be priced out in pence – a conservative estimate would be tenths of a penny per hour of use. To add how highly I value some of the views I have had through them, the happy times with friends, birds I have seen for the first time, records of new species of dragonflies for our reserve and much more, they become almost priceless.

How to use binoculars

It is worth practising when you get your first pair of binoculars as it is surprisingly easy to have lost your target during the process of lifting them up to your eyes, especially when there are no points of reference, such as when you are looking at a bird in flight above you. Practice is therefore essential.

Take a little time to practise on any object, a flower in the garden, a plane passing overhead. This will help to ensure that when you lift your binoculars to your eyes to catch that fleeting glimpse of something promising you will get on to it immediately. Half a second may be the difference between seeing your bird and missing it.

Exercise

Pick a target object. With your binoculars in your hands, lift them to your eyes without taking your eyes off the object. Obviously as they pass in front of your eyes they will obscure your view, but if your eyes stay looking in the right direction when the binoculars come into position you should be on your target.

An easy mistake to make, costing you valuable time, is that as your binoculars obscure your view when you lift them up, you look into them and your eyes come 'off target'. A bout of wandering view through the binoculars usually follows until you find your target again, by which time of course it might have gone.

The other thing to get familiar with is the focus wheel. Good binoculars should go through a full range from closest to infinity in a couple of turns. In the same way that you want your binoculars to be pointing at your target immediately, you also want your bird to be in focus as quickly as possible. So try putting your binoculars out of focus, then bringing them up to your eyes and focusing them on your chosen object. This will ensure that you get in the habit of turning the focus wheel the right way. Focus on an object that is close to, then an object in the distance, and vice versa.

Once you have been using your binoculars for a while and they are a good fit, looking through them will seem second nature. But don't spend all your time with them glued to your face. They do magnify things beautifully but they also reduce the field of view, the amount of things you can see, significantly. Your eyes are optically superb and you should maximize your chances of finding things worth a closer look by using your eyes and ears primarily and your technical equipment next. On more than one occasion I have watched people walk into a hide, sit down and immediately bring their binoculars up and start to scan the area; meanwhile a Kingfisher whizzes past under their noses, an interesting Warbler is feeding on a nearby branch or even once a fantastic view of a Firecrest was so close to hand that binoculars wouldn't have been necessary. Often these luckless people would round off their all too brief scan of the area by stating that, 'There's nothing out there'. Use your binoculars to add detail, not as an appendage to your eyes.

Here are a few tips to help you choose the right pair of binoculars for you and some of the key criteria the quality of binoculars are assessed against.

Buying binoculars

- Your binoculars are personal to you: the size of your hands, your strength and the shape of your face are all unique to you. Different binoculars suit different people; you absolutely must try before you buy. Many good retailers offer field days where you can enjoy the expert advice of their staff and try a number of pairs of binoculars side by side for comparison.
- Do your research. Birdwatching magazines and websites are full of independent reviews and the manufacturers' own

websites and marketing material will have technical specifications of their products.

- Ideally try them out as the light is fading at the end of the day or in poor, dull weather (a great thing to do on a rainy day!). Really good quality optics will perform much better in poor light; the difference between 'Okay' and 'superb' is much harder to spot in bright, ideal conditions.

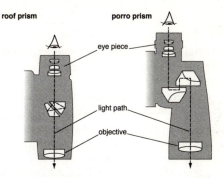

figure 17 roof and porro prism binoculars

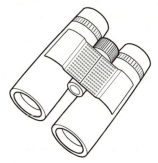

figure 18 roof prism binoculars

figure 19 porro prism binoculars

Roof prism or porro prism

Roof prism binoculars are the straight design. They are generally thought to be better than porro prism (the rounded design) although these are usually lighter and cheaper. There are some good value porro prism binoculars at the lower end of the market. They also feel different in your hands, being a different shape so you may find one design more comfortable than the other.

Magnification

The greater the magnification the narrower the field of view and the less light is transmitted through the optic. Higher magnifications also cause any small shake or movement of your hand to be magnified, which can blur the image and negate any benefit of the subject image being larger.

The most popular magnification for birdwatching is 8× as this is thought to be the ideal balance between magnification power, image quality and ease of handling. Also popular is 10× and with higher quality binoculars the optics will be so good that they will still produce an excellent bright image (although you should be sure that you can hold this magnification steady as some people do not feel they can).

Weight

See 'Brightness' on page 61. The most important thing to bear in mind when trying out binoculars is that you will be carrying them for much longer periods of time than when you try them before buying. If they feel heavy after a few minutes consider how they will feel after a few hours' use. There is no point at all in having them tucked away in your bag. They must be in your hand or hanging round your neck to be of any use at all. Binoculars that are too heavy will also be difficult to hold steady.

Close focus

Most binoculars focus down to two or three metres away. You will want to see detail this close on birds, or even just enhance a pleasurable view. Close focus really becomes essential if and when you find yourself getting interested in other groups of wild animals, particularly butterflies and dragonflies. If you start to become interested in these fascinating insects you will be very frustrated when your binoculars do not focus close enough to afford a magnified view of them.

Coated optics

Obviously the quality of the optics is very significant in delivering a clear, bright image and you should look for glass that is multi-coated; these coatings maximize the light coming through the glass to your eye and all good binoculars will have some degree of multi-coating. Pay special attention to the quality of the image and the edge of the field of view; good optics will stay sharp all the way to the edge.

Image sharpness

Assess the resolution of the image the binoculars provide by looking at something with a distinct, tight pattern. The vermiculation on a duck is an excellent test. Vermiculation is what makes up grey on most ducks' plumage – they are not actually grey at all but have very closely arranged black and white stripes. Alternatively you could look at a bar code on some packaging or some small text on a page. Try checking a straight edge such as a telegraph pole or building. Look at this with the edge of the image, if it distorts then the prism quality is deficient.

Brightness

I have often been looking for birds on our reserve when it is too dark to see. The light gathering quality of my binoculars can show up things I didn't know were there. The objective lens relative to the magnification dictates how bright your binoculars are.

The popular objective size for binoculars is 42 mm, so the most popular specification will be written as 8×42. As with magnification this is a compromise between brightness and ease of use. Larger objectives are heavier, so if you feel more comfortable with a lighter pair you may want to go for 32 mm. Manufacturers are constantly trying to improve the optical quality of their 32 mm binoculars and make 42 mm lighter to gain a competitive advantage in their market.

Magnification is important when considering brightness as a higher magnification requires a larger objective lens to maintain the same brightness.

Image quality

No binoculars present an image of such quality as your naked eye; the binoculars' image travels through lenses which distort it to some degree. The trick is to get the distortion as small as possible. To assess the degree of 'fringing' a particular optic presents, look at a dark object against a light background – the top branches of a tree or a tall lamp post against the sky can work, anything that is small and dark. You are looking for any colour fringing to the object you are looking at.

Depth of field

The more you can see clearly without turning your focus wheel the better. The depth of field is how much is sharp enough to see clearly in front and behind the point of focus. Focus on a mid-point in a long view and then see how much is clear close to and far away.

Field of view

The greater the field of view the more you get to see! Field of view is measured as width at 1,000 metres. This is a difficult thing for you to measure but you should be able to get this data from the manufacturer's own website or independent reviews.

Fit

Fit is how they feel in your hands and on your face; there may especially be a difference in fit between men and women. You must be able to reach the focus wheel comfortably. Spectacle wearers should make sure that the retractable eye cups work well to give enough eye relief to fit well with glasses on. When the binoculars are brought up to your eyes in a comfortable position you should be seeing the whole field of view.

Cost

As long as you have followed the advice in this chapter, buy the best you can afford. Binoculars made by reputable manufacturers for the birding market are generally all excellent and provide good value. Don't worry if you can't afford the best, choose carefully and you can expect years of good birding with entry level binoculars. If you are on a budget you may also want to look at good quality second-hand optics.

Guarantee

Most quality optics are guaranteed for ten years or more.

Accessories

Even the lightest binoculars can feel heavy around your neck after a while. A good quality, wide, soft neoprene strap is an essential investment. Unless your binoculars come with a really comfortable strap like this (many of the higher priced models do) you should not put up with the manufacturer's own but buy a more comfortable one straight away. Many vendors will throw one in free as a sweetener for a sale. You may also want to have a look at the harness style of strap which spreads weight even more than a broad strap.

Most binoculars come with a 'rain' guard. You can buy these as separate items and they are another essential piece of kit. They stay attached to the strap of your binoculars and protect your eyecups from all sorts of debris: rain, sandwich crumbs and bits of plants to name a few. For obvious reasons it is best to prevent these items from filling your eye cups and obscuring your view. All rain guards should protect your binoculars, the difference between the ones that work best and not so well is the speed and ease with which you can take them on and off.

Clothing

I have discussed clothing in some detail in Chapter 06. To summarize:

- Be prepared to get hotter, colder or wetter than you think you might. Even in summer don't assume that what looks like dry ground on a map won't turn out to be swamp when you get there.
- Birding is 'stop/start', so wear layers to stay comfortable when tramping around with a heavy telescope and tripod which can be removed when you're hot and put back on when you stop and watch.
- Rustling clothing is a drag for you and those around you. The less noise your clothes make, the more chance you have of hearing the birds and wildlife around you. Consider treated cotton fabrics or maybe old-fashioned waxed jackets as some modern fabrics can make quite a noise.

- Birds see UV light, so what looks drab to us may not look drab to the birds. Whether bright colours disturb birds or not, they usually disturb people enjoying the countryside. I personally think the birds will see you whatever you wear but you're best to dress in muted colours anyway. The way you move is probably more important.

Telescope

I will not dwell too much on telescopes here. Being a piece of optical equipment, many of the qualities I have listed for binoculars also apply to telescopes. Larger objective lenses let in more light but make the telescope heavier; greater magnification will reduce the field of view and brightness and will increase any wobble. Depth of field and image quality should also be considered.

The main point is that telescopes can be expensive and a relatively heavy piece of kit to carry around. As your interest in birding grows you will definitely want one. If you can afford one by all means buy one as soon as you like, but don't miss the chance to see birds because you are too busy setting your scope up. Get to see as much as you can to start with, get really comfortable using your binoculars – they will help you see a lot of birds. The value you will get from a scope is great but nothing like what you will get from your binoculars. In certain habitats and settings a telescope is very useful, if not essential, but don't be put off if you don't feel you can afford one just yet. Other birders in hides or at gatherings to see rare birds will often offer you the chance to view a bird through their scope and many nature reserves have scopes permanently set up for visitors to use.

If you do feel you can afford one straight away, or you have reached a point in your birdwatching where you want to see that little bit further, or to be able to see a little more detail in a Waders plumage, for example, here are a few things to consider when choosing a scope. Do also bear in mind the general principles on optics outlined in the previous section on binoculars.

Magnification

You have two main choices in magnification: fixed magnification (usually wide angle) or zoom. The most popular wide angle lens is a ×30wa and the most popular zoom range is

×20–×60. Zoom lenses are usually thought of as producing a less high quality image but the top quality telescopes today are so good that a zoom will still produce superb images, at any magnification. Wide angle lenses are cheaper and produce very good image quality.

Straight or angled

Most people use a scope with an angled body. Straight scopes can be easier to aim at your target bird but angled are generally more comfortable to use in a greater range of situations. See figures 21 and 22 overleaf.

If more than one person wants to look down the same scope (something that happens a lot) an angled scope means that people of different heights can look down the same scope more easily without changing the height of the tripod. Generally, an angled scope makes more efficient use of the available space for your head, body and gear combined, so you fit into hides and cars better while you are looking down your scope.

Angled scopes can be comfortably used for looking at Raptors and other birds in flight, or birds in the tops of trees, down to birds on the ground. To do this with a straight scope is much more difficult.

Angled scopes do not have to be set as high, so you can get away with a smaller, lighter weight tripod, or set your tripod lower for a steadier support.

It is personal choice but most people choose angled bodies on scopes.

Size of objective lens

There is no point spending the best part of a thousand pounds on something you leave at home because it is too big and heavy to carry. Many people prefer a smaller scope and manufacturers have responded to this by producing slightly smaller, lighter scopes that still have absolutely superb optical quality. Scopes and binoculars are getting lighter all the time as manufacturers develop new technology and employ new materials. Most scopes have objective lenses of around 60–65 mm or 80–85 mm. There are also much smaller scopes that can be a lot cheaper and are becoming increasingly popular as technology improves.

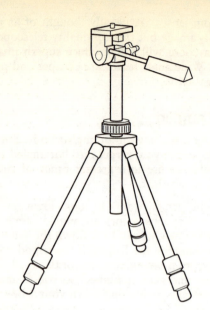

figure 20 tripod

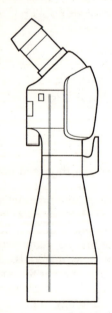

figure 21 angled body scope

figure 22 straight body scope

> **Top tip**
>
> One of the drawbacks of using a telescope is that you only use one eye at a time. You may find that your closed eye gets quite tired if you are using your telescope for any length of time, especially if doing any sea watching or Raptor watching. Leaving the unused eye open can work well. Concentrate on the image in the other eye; with practice this can be useful if you are making notes at the same time as looking down your scope. Some people cut a piece of foam large enough to cover both eyes, then make a hole in one side to fit snugly over the lens of the scope. When they then look through the scope the unused eye will be shielded and will not produce a confusing second image. A more extreme option when doing extended sea watching is to wear an eye patch.

Inside information

Once you start to get confident with your birding and are becoming familiar with your garden birds, local patch and many of the more common birds you will find in different habitats, you may want the chance to see some rarer birds, or even just get up-to-date news on the first arrival of migrants and more information from around your country or region.

Many of us have access to the internet today and it is an excellent source of information about birds and birdwatching. There are also many sites that list bird news, especially rarities (see Taking it Further, at the end of the book for details).

If you are really keen and want to maximize your chances of seeing rare birds in your area, there are a number of 'Bird Alert' services. These can be email, SMS text message, pager or phone based. Almost all require a subscription fee but there will also be a considerable amount of news available for free.

Bird ID videos, DVD-Roms, CD-Roms, audio CDs and even multi-media guides for handheld computers are all excellent aids to learning and reference for identification.

The following are some suggested websites and magazines to get you started:

www.fatbirder.com
www.surfbirds.com
www.bbc.co.uk/nature/animals/birds

www.arkive.org
www.rspb.org.uk
www.bto.org
www.wwt.org.uk
www.wildlifetrusts.org.uk

Birdwatch magazine
Birdwatching magazine
BBC Wildlife magazine

Photographing birds

Photographing birds is a very enjoyable and popular activity and can be an extension to your birdwatching. It is not considered here, as it warrants a book in its own right. Digiscoping is the term used for taking digital images using a camera (or mobile picture phone) and your telescope. It is possible to obtain good quality images that benefit from the high magnification of your scope. These images will not be as good as those taken with an SLR (single lens reflex) camera but they can be very good. I will not go further into digiscoping here, my aim is simply to make you aware that it is an option for you to explore, or not, at some later date. If you choose to have a go, you will need:

- a telescope (on a tripod obviously)
- a digital camera
- a means to attach the two together – many camera and telescope manufacturers produce these gadgets
- patience.

There is loads of material in magazines and on the web about digiscoping to help you get started.

getting birds to come to you

In this chapter you will learn:
- how to attract birds to your garden
- different types of bird food
- how to provide shelter for birds
- what a 'local patch' is and why you should find one.

Wildlife gardening and birds in your garden

Whether you are new to watching birds or have been doing it for many years and have become quite expert, the birds in your garden, on your windowsill and around your home will always provide special interest. If you are lucky enough to have a garden, allotment or other land, you have the opportunity to 'manage' the environment somewhat in order to benefit wildlife and to ensure that you get to see what's there. Don't worry if you don't have a garden, there is still a lot you can do to attract birds to a windowsill, and whether you are in town or country you should always be able to find a 'local patch' (I'll explain more about this later in the chapter) that will provide very rewarding birding.

Birds are very different to us in many ways, but there is one common theme that we share: we are both warm-blooded animals. As such we need water, food and shelter. Without these things we would perish; where these things are in good supply we should thrive.

Food for birds can be thought of in two categories: firstly, artificially provided food, prepared or bought by yourself and put out for birds; secondly, a food-rich habitat that you have provided by the way you plant and organize your garden or other space, perhaps by leaving some rough meadow for insects, an open compost heap or planting berry- or seed-producing plants.

Similarly, shelter can be thought of in natural and manmade categories. Probably the easiest, most productive (for your birds) and entertaining (for you) shelter you can provide is nesting boxes that mimic natural shelter, like a box with a small hole which recreates a cavity in an old tree for nesting Tits (or Chickadees if you're in the US). Of course, different birds favour different areas to nest and roost, so providing natural shelter by allowing a corner of the garden to become overgrown with brambles or planting some hedgerow can also be of tremendous value to birds and wildlife.

If you do not have a garden or any outdoor space of your own you can still encourage birds to come close enough for really good views. Walls provide the opportunity to hang feeders or even place a nest box. However, remember that birds that are adapted to life in the low cover of woodland edge such as Blue Tits may not fly up high enough to find peanut feeders hung

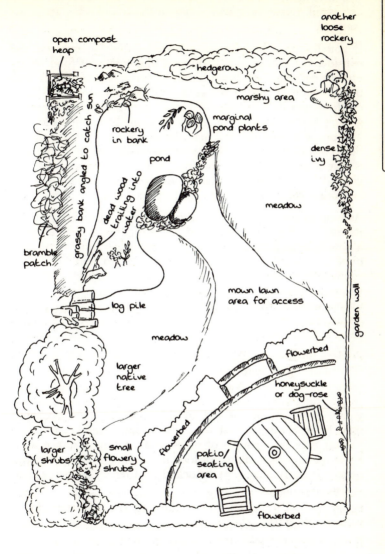

figure 23 a good wildlife garden layout

from tall buildings. Think about the types of habitat and birds you have nearby and cater for them as you are more likely to be successful. Experiment with different foods and other attractive features.

If you live in a building with people living beneath you, do consider the risk of bird droppings and scraps of food falling onto or past their windows. It may be better to get together with other residents and propose a feeding station in a shared outdoor area like a garden or patio – they may find themselves getting as interested as you are in watching birds and as long as it is properly planned and maintained a feeding station should be no trouble to anyone. If the wrong feeders are used, the area is not regularly cleaned, or food left inappropriately on the ground the resulting droppings, visits from rats, feral pigeons and other pests could cause inconvenience or worse.

As long as you have thought about the type of feeders you are putting out, always persevere. When you put up a new feeder or a new type of food to your existing feeding station it can take quite some time for the birds in the area to find it, become comfortable with it and begin using it regularly. Birds are uncomfortable about change. A cautious approach usually makes sense in the wild. Similarly, if you stop filling up your feeding station for a while (I recommend you keep it well stocked year round) it may take some time for the birds to come back.

Feeding birds in the spring and summer is important, especially for adult birds who are too busy feeding young to feed themselves properly. Many people wrongly think they should stop feeding at this time of year. You will see birds come for the winter but stay right through till the young have fledged, when they bring these to feed too. The nearest suitable breeding habitat may be a couple of miles away, a long distance for a Passerine to come looking for food in breeding season. They will benefit from finding a well-stocked bird feeder on every visit, throughout the year.

Don't give up if you have the right food for the right birds in your area and they are still not using it after a couple of weeks. It can sometimes take time. However, don't allow food to turn bad. It is better to throw away and replace food than to leave old or rotten food in feeders.

Types of artificial food

Insectivorous birds have beaks adapted for catching and eating insects. You can provide live or freeze-dried insect food for wild birds. I will discuss this in more detail later on. This may be expensive and present trickier storage issues than artificial foods that likewise meet the needs of insectivorous birds. Although many can exploit some seeds as a source of food they are generally attracted to artificial foods that are high in energy, fatty foods, and foods that are soft enough to peck at or tear small pieces off.

Providing food for seed-eating birds is fairly straightforward. Just put out seeds that are similar to those they eat in the wild. These can be put out in hanging feeders that provide perches for the birds. Keep the food clean and dry and prevent any pests from getting at it. Many seed-eating birds prefer to eat on the ground so you may want to scatter some food directly on the ground or on another flat surface such as a bird table, either hanging or on a stand.

Possibly the best all-round food for cleanliness, ease of presenting at the feeding station and attractiveness to the broadest range of species is the peanut. Peanuts can be provided with their husks still on, or more usually as loose peanuts contained in a hanging cage or net bag. Some birds such as Jays may be attracted to loose peanuts so these may be worth scattering around too. Most pet shops and garden centres sell suitable varieties, as do a number of internet-based mail order retailers. Suitable ones will come with an industry standard guarantee. They should be untreated; keep the dry roasted and salted varieties for yourself. Peanuts are particularly attractive to insectivorous birds as they are so energy rich, relatively soft and when you hang them in a cage you are really creating an artificial tree with rich insect grubs hidden in the bark. Birds such as Tits are well adapted to hanging and climbing on vertical surfaces and pecking at fatty little morsels. For the same reason you may be lucky enough to attract Woodpeckers and Nuthatches to your garden by putting out peanut feeders.

figure 24 hanging seed feeder

figure 25 hanging feeder

figure 26 hanging peanut feeder

figure 27 squirrel proof peanut feeder

figure 28 stick-on-window feeder

figure 29 ground feeder

Insectivorous birds also eat other energy-rich foods. Another commonly available hanging food is the 'fat ball'. These comprise some food stuff, normally seed, in a ball of suet and are hung in a net bag or metal feeder. The best thing about fat balls is that as well as being good for attracting birds to the garden, you can easily make your own if you have time. Take some left-over bread, suitable kitchen scraps (like seeds, nuts, dried fruit, oatmeal – nothing that will turn bad), then melt some suet in a pan and add your ingredients. Mix it thoroughly and either leave it to cool in a cake tin or as it cools roll it into balls and allow it to set.

Probably the premium food for insectivorous birds is live insect food or freeze-dried insects. This is especially attractive to birds in the spring when they are feeding young and the need to find quality high-protein food is paramount. Young fledgling birds may also appreciate live animal food as they still have lots of growing to do once they leave the nest. These 'live foods' are available from pet shops and mail order companies, are relatively expensive, difficult to present without them escaping and difficult to store when compared with other alternatives. But the birds will love them and you may be able to enjoy really close views of birds that otherwise would not come to your feeding station. The most common live food is beetle grubs, sometimes called 'meal worms'. They are the easiest type of live food to keep and feed as they don't move around much, normally come with their own food source in their container and as long as they are kept in a cool place they last quite well and need little maintenance. Obviously the big challenge with live food is allowing the birds to get at it while preventing it from running away (crickets and locusts are widely available as live food but are not so good for birds as they tend to hop away as soon as they are put out!). This is achieved by placing the food in steep-sided dishes that are sheltered from rain. Most of the main suppliers of bird food also supply special live food feeders.

Although seed-eating birds like Finches eat peanuts and may even hang on the side of a peanut feeder in the way Tits do, you will attract a greater variety and number of seed-eating birds if you put out specific seed feeders as well as peanuts and other food. A variety of different seeds can be bought for different birds, or you can buy a mixture. Most people feed either sunflower seeds or a mix of different seeds. Hanging seed feeders are available, very similar to the hanging wire cage peanut feeders, and are excellent. One thing to bear in mind with seed is that the reason certain species are able to exploit this food source and others can't is that birds like Finches have adapted to strip the husk from the seed. This is a hard protective outer layer and has little nutritional value so the bird discards it. At a busy feeding station the accumulation of empty sunflower seed husks and other detritous can build up quite quickly. Some hanging feeders have trays that can be attached to the underneath of them to catch any waste. Alternatively, if you want to keep things looking tidy you can buy seed ready husked which, although more expensive, may reduce the amount of waste on the ground by your feeders.

If you have the space experiment with different seeds in different feeders and see which species favour which foods. One special type of seed to look out for is Niger seed, which is excellent for attracting small Finches like Goldfinch.

Bird food should be stored in the same way that other dried foods would be kept. Do not keep food for excessive periods and ensure it is stored in a cool, dry environment or as the supplier recommends. Bird food can be bought cheaper in large quantities but this may be a false economy if you do not go through it very quickly. Food should always be fairly fresh and never mouldy or musty.

It is essential you keep your feeders and feeding area clean. With a large number of birds feeding in such a small space the chance of disease being spread is very high as droppings may accumulate on feeding surfaces. Food that has gone off may also cause harm to your birds. Clean hanging feeders thoroughly with hot water every time you refill them and if you feed on a flat table clean it every day with a detergent that is safe for animals (a pet shop may be able to supply safe products). If you put food loose on the ground or you have ground-feeding birds enjoying the bits of seed and peanut dropped by birds on the hanging feeders, move the feeding station around regularly, every week or two if you can. This should be easy to do if you have a free-standing table or hanging feeders on poles. Apart from the harm it causes the wild bird population, it is really sad to see the birds you love to watch every day becoming sick and dying through poor hygiene on our part.

Siting of feeders, pests and predators

Site your feeders where you can get a good view of them, as often as possible. Outside the sitting room window, or anywhere you spend some time is ideal because you do want to see them as much as you can.

This is also very good for the birds. Sparrowhawks will be attracted to garden bird feeders because of the density of potential prey, but the way that Sparrowhawks hunt is usually to slip low and fast, hidden behind bushes before flicking over onto their startled prey at the last minute. No fair chase with a Sparrowhawk, no advance warning, this bird is always a surprise attack. Similarly your neighbourhood cats (maybe they are your own?) would never outrun a bird in a straight contest; they need the element of surprise to catch their prey (except they don't need to catch anything because they are probably so well fed their tummies are almost dragging an the ground!).

You will benefit both the birds and yourself if you set a bird feeding station up in plain view, well away from any cover – or at least far enough away so that your wild birds can see someone or something coming. Some statistics suggest that the number of birds being killed by domestic cats in England is between half a million and 1 million a year, which seems very conservative and may have been based on a fairly crude study.

Tips for deterring cats from birds:

- One of the oldest is to place a bell on the cat's collar. A cat is unlikely to outpace a bird and they tend to go from still to pouncing ambush. Bells don't jangle when they're still, when the cat pounces it is too late.
- Make potential ambush points less attractive to cats by placing prickly cuttings in and around them. Cats like to skulk under shrubbery and wait to ambush birds and small mammals. If you have spread holly leaves, bramble trimmings, gorse, hawthorn or other similar cuttings around these areas it will prevent cats from getting comfortably settled there and keep them out in the open where the birds can see them coming.
- Continuing on the subject of spikes, there are specifically designed metal wrap arounds for trees and feeding stations that prevent cats and other less desirable animals from climbing up them. They pose no threat to the cat but prevent it from climbing up to get at the birds. These devices are made up of links that can be added or taken out so will fit a variety of different trees or other upright structures.
- There are also protective devices that you can place on the entrance hole of your bird boxes. These make it harder for predators to reach in with a paw or claw to harm the eggs, young and adults inside. They may also provide some protection to the adults as they fly in and out of the box on feeding trips.

- No animals like to be sprayed with a water pistol. It will deter cats and is a humane enough deterrent to be widely regarded as an acceptable thing to do when training dogs out of bad habits. There are electronically controlled deterrents that detect a large animal in your garden and spray water for a couple of seconds! If you don't want to invest in such technological gadgets you could always just turn the sprinkler on for a minute whenever you see a neighbourhood cat.
- Another type of electronic deterrent emit ultrasonic sound. Apparently these can be calibrated so that some only disturb cats and no other animals, and some deter a wider range of mammals. I have not tried one of these but have read mixed reviews in the past.
- Keep dogs!

Squirrels

Grey squirrels are classed as a pest in the UK. They are not a native species to the islands and they can cause problems. They eat birds' eggs and young from time to time, they may possibly outcompete the native red squirrel. If they nest in your house they may chew electrical cabling and make holes in your roof and, worst of all, they will do their best to destroy bird feeders in their quest for peanuts.

If you live in an area where there is a grey squirrel population buy feeders that are protected by a metal cage and are made of metal. Squirrels will destroy cheaper plastic feeders and you will end up buying metal ones anyway.

Another way to prevent squirrels having access to your feeders is to attach a specially designed hanging 'roof' above free-hanging feeders; these are available from the same companies that manufacture the feeders themselves. Or, if you have free-standing feeders on poles, buy a dish (which usually screws into the bottom of the feeder) to prevent squirrels climbing up the pole to the food, which also catches seed husks and other scraps, providing another surface for birds to feed on that is also easy to keep clean.

The most novel way of deterring squirrels is to dust the bird food with capsicum pepper powder. For useful evolutionary reasons or by accident, birds do not feel the chilli pepper heat the way mammals do. The chilli powder does the birds no harm at all but the squirrels will find it unpalatable and will leave the food alone. This powder is often sold by bird food manufacturers under brand names such as 'Squirrel Away' but it all does the same thing.

Rats

Rats spread disease that is contagious to humans and although all rodents, even small mice, are capable of damaging your house, rats and squirrels can do a serious job quickly. If you are feeding birds and either rats or squirrels are present, feed on poles (most feeders are adapted to be mounted on special poles) and use caged feeders. If, like me, you want to attract some species of bird that only like to feed on the ground, put the food in a ground cage so that rats can't access the food at night.

I have said this before, but I think it is so important I'll say it again. Clean your feeding station. Clean table surfaces daily. If you feed on the ground move the location of your feeding to prevent birds from eating each others faeces and clean hanging feeders every time you fill them. If they aren't attracting many birds throw old food away, clean them and fill with fresh.

Natural food sources

Good natural sources of food can be provided in the garden by planting berry-bearing shrubs. The following are good examples:

- holly
- pyracantha
- cotoneaster
- berberis
- viburnum
- snowberry
- elder
- hawthorn
- teasel
- sunflower.

Also, leaving some brambles in a corner provides both cover and a source of food. If you have any fruit trees leave some apples or other fruit on the top of the tree for birds and insects to eat. Birds will eat windfall fruit even when it is breaking down and rotting. Some birds have an enzyme in their digestive systems that enables them to eat fermenting fruit without suffering the effects of alcohol – so you'll never see a drunk Starling no matter how many fermenting apples they have eaten!

If you have space to let some meadow grow up, don't mow it but cut it after the seed has set (flowers have been and gone and seed heads have turned brown and withered), let it lie on the ground and rake it up. This should allow much of the seed from the grasses and flowering plants to drop and will provide new plants next year as well as a source of food for the birds through autumn and winter. If you have the space (i.e. your garden is like a small field) you could even sow some cereal crops in an unused corner and allow the seed to lie over the autumn and winter.

Other good sources of food for wild birds include open compost heaps (or just open on one side if you want to keep things reasonably tidy). A good way of making a fairly open compost heap is to use discarded wooden pallets for the four sides with wooden stakes hammered into the ground to support them. This contains your compost but leaves space through the slatted sides and from the top for all sorts of things to get in. Piles of logs and rotting wood are excellent for insects and therefore good for birds.

Obviously anything that is bad for insects and other invertebrates will be bad for any animals that feed on them, either by directly poisoning the animal eating the invertebrate or just because the poison kills the invertebrates and there are therefore fewer invertebrates to eat. If you value your wildlife it is best to use organic gardening methods and not put down any poisonous insecticide. Herbicides should be used only when absolutely necessary and after you have really thought through the short- and long-term impacts.

Artificial shelter

Different designs of nest box meet the needs of a wide range of different species of bird, mainly by mimicking the design of a natural nest or nesting cavity or platform. As with providing food, if you put up nest boxes for species that do not occur in your area you may be frustrated or at least be in for a long wait. Fortunately most of the common nest boxes are fairly generic and will attract a range of common species with considerable chance of success. If, for example, you have Swifts in your area it may well be worth the trouble of putting up more specialized nesting boxes for them, as they are extraordinary birds. Interestingly, they are one of the species that, having originally nested high up in dead trees, has now adapted to nest almost exclusively on the eaves of buildings and is inextricably linked to the presence of man and his built environment.

General principles for siting nest boxes are:

- Never place your nesting boxes near your feeding station.
- The most common nest boxes should be placed about 170 cm above ground level to deter predators and appeal to your birds. Other, more specialist nesting boxes can be placed much higher (boxes for Owls, for example, or for Swifts and Swallows which should be above 6 metres).
- Nesting boxes should generally face south-east as this provides the most sheltered aspect and they should not be in direct sunlight. The thicker and more robust the build of your boxes, the less this may matter.
- In an average size garden put up four or five boxes. The small tree-hole type are the most likely to be used but you may want to try a mix. If you find that all the nesting boxes are occupied it would be worth putting up some more until you find that they are at a density where some are not used. If you have Swifts, Martins and Swallows nesting in special boxes on your house this should not affect the number of tree hole and platform nesting birds in the garden as their choice of nesting location and ecology differ so greatly.

'Tree hole' boxes – small

Chance of success: High.

Potential range of species attracted: Medium to high.

figure 30 small tree hole box

If peanuts are the premier food for your wild birds, the small 'tree hole' nest box is the number one design for successfully attracting a number of birds to bring up their family in your garden. There are no longer sufficient numbers of old and dead trees standing around with rotten or hollow cores or wood soft enough to excavate a hole in. Our gardens, as a rule, tend to represent a woodland edge habitat, so the birds of woodland edges and clearings thrive in our company. In the UK these are the mainly the Tits but you may attract Nuthatches or Tree Sparrows as well. By hanging a nest box with a hole in the front from a tree you are mimicking a tree with a hole in its structure.

Swift and Hirundine (Swallows and House Martins) 'cups'

Chance of success: Low to medium, depending on whether these species already nest in your locality.

Potential range of species attracted: Low, unless they are already in your neighbourhood.

Swifts live in the air. If they could nest on clouds they would. They feed in the air on aerial insects, they sleep in the air, they mate in the air, they pick up wet mud to make their nests from the air (although they prefer to take over old, disused hirundine nests), they fly up and down our planet to ensure the best conditions for breeding and the best supply of flying insects. And they have adapted to make use of our built environment; apparently Swifts do still nest in the tops of old trees. However, as a rule, they almost all now nest in mud cups they create on our buildings.

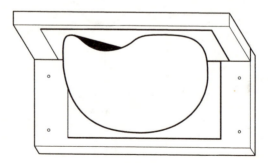

figure 31 House Martin cup

These types of birds tend to favour their ancestral breeding sites and also like to nest communally. If you want to encourage these birds, think you have suitable buildings and know these birds frequent your area it is probably worth trying more than one box (or cup).

One of the best things about species of Martin, Swallow and Swift is that as their nest boxes need to be placed under eaves of buildings, they can easily be placed near an upstairs window and you can watch them coming and going all spring and summer.

These boxes should be placed above 6 metres. As with other boxes, they should face away from the worst weather and direct sunlight.

As these boxes are placed directly on your house you should consider where the droppings from the young may land. They don't make a lot of mess but it isn't terribly pleasant, especially when they may rear two or three broods in a season.

Communal nesters (Sparrows)

Chance of success: High if you have sparrows in the area.

Potential range of species attracted: Low to medium (if you don't get communal nesters side by side you may still get a more private species using just one compartment).

House Sparrows and some other species like to nest close to each other. The House Sparrow is in decline in the UK for reasons not fully understood. If you have these noisy, social and

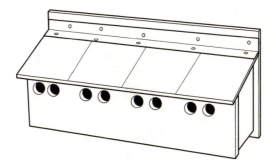

figure 32 House Sparrow box

charismatic little birds in your area, one thing you can do to help them is to provide good quality shelter for breeding. If you are successful in attracting them to breed in your garden, because they are communal you will obviously get more than one pair together. The potential for watching their entertaining comings and goings is huge.

'Tree hole' boxes – large (Owls, Woodpeckers)

Chance of success: Low as these birds are less common and have larger territories.

Potential range of species attracted: Medium to low.

As with the common smaller tree hole nesters, opportunities for birds to excavate or find suitable holes in dead or old trees is

figure 33 large barn owl box

figure 34 large tree hole nester

plate 1 Blue Tit

plate 2 Gannet

plate 3 Whooper Swan

plate 4 Sedge Warbler

plate 5 Little Grebe

plate 6 Robin

plate 7 Blackbird

plate 8 Greenfinch

plate 9 Wood pigeon

plate 10 Long-tailed tit

plate 11 Whitethroat

plate 12 Mandarin Duck

plate 13 Bewick's Swan

plate 14 Black-headed Gull

plate 15 Buzzard in flight

plate 16 Sparrowhawk

plate 17 Tufted Duck

greatly limited in today's world. By providing an equivalent cavity on the side of a tree or building you have a chance of attracting some very exciting birds to nest in your area, especially if you live on a large property or farm. It may also be possible to sight nest boxes on adjacent land, or on or near your local patch, although obviously you would need the landowner's permission. Organizations like the Hawk and Owl Trust work with landowners to place Owl nesting boxes in suitable locations and these can meet with considerable success.

One of the most underrated birds in the UK (and unfortunately the US too; a few hundred were introduced to Central Park in New York some years ago – they now number in the millions and may have a negative impact on the native fauna) is the Starling. As so happens with many common birds I saw them, instantly recognized them and quickly went on to look at other 'more interesting' birds without having really observed them. When I realized how interesting and important it was to learn the songs and calls of birds I noticed the Starlings singing from the roof of my parents' house. The range of crackling trills and clicks, whistles and mimicry is captivating. And then when you see one close up; their plumage is so beautiful, dark, oily petrol colours and a very handsome, proud bird. And when you see the vast flocks of them going into a winter roost, whether you find birds interesting or not, it is a breathtaking sight. Starlings are tree hole nesters and will nest in a box similar to that of the Tits. Obviously they are bigger so the box and hole needs to be bigger (see figure 34) but otherwise they are similar and if you have these common but wonderful birds in your area the chance of the boxes being occupied by a pair are high.

Less likely hole nesters may be worth taking the chance on because they are just so exciting. Woodpeckers, Nuthatches, Treecreepers and Owls are the most likely candidates from the slightly more unusual list of birds that could be helped to find a place to breed on your property. As with other birds these species have specific requirements and need a design and sighting of box that suits their needs – Woodpeckers and Owls need a very much larger and different design than other birds you may attract.

The last two designs are lovely and the birds they attract are charming. These designs are quite specialist and may only be available from one or two companies.

Hanging Wren house

figure 35 Wren nest house

Chance of success: Medium.

Potential range of species attracted: Low (Wrens are small and only birds as small as Wrens can get in).

The scientific name for the Wren is *Troglodytes troglodytes*, which means cave dweller. They do not live in caves, but they do have a habit of poking around in little nooks and crannies in their search for insect food. Wrens are brilliant little birds and appear constantly active. Although a rusty brown in colour they are very attractive and their distinctive song is one of the most commonly heard and the loudest. You should take the trouble to learn it early on.

And the best bit; they are Britain's commonest bird. Our parks, gardens, woodlands and countryside are awash with these stunning little birds.

Tree creeper box

Chance of success: Medium to low.

Potential range of species attracted: Low, only likely to attract Treecreepers and maybe small mammals and insects.

Treecreepers are, as the name suggests, a woodland specialist. They climb up the trunks of trees like little brown mice with white bellies, picking invertebrates from the crevices in the bark with their delicate down-curved beak.

They have a number of interesting habits, including roosting pressed into a hollow on a tree trunk; their camouflage allows them to blend perfectly against the trunk and they sleep there all night.

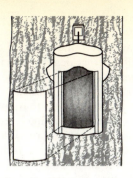

figure 36 treecreeper box

Because of their climbing habit, they like a nest box that they can climb into from the trunk side rather than a hole in the front.

Different materials – wood, woodcrete, ceramic, woven

You will come across bird boxes and feeders in a wide range of different materials. Probably the most popular are wood and a specially designed material called 'woodcrete'. The latter is arguably the premium material for nest boxes and manufacturers claim results of tests that show higher occupation rates than other materials. I have not subjected these materials to such rigorous tests but 'woodcrete' boxes are always popular with garden birds.

Making your own boxes can be fun and a lot cheaper than buying them. There are loads of designs available in books and on the internet. The two things to consider when choosing the wood you are going to use are:

1 How well insulated will the box be once you have finished? A stable temperature is paramount for successful occupation and breeding by birds.
2 Will your box be robust enough to withstand predators? Squirrels and Woodpeckers are among the many animals that will seek to feed themselves and their own young with the eggs and young of other birds. Squirrels have formidable gnawing powers, so a thicker, more robust construction is usually best.

Water

Creating a wetland area or pond in your garden will benefit birds and other wildlife a great deal by providing somewhere to drink and bathe as well as a rich habitat for insects and other animals. If you have enough space and can create a big enough pond or other wetland you may find that you attract birds that specialize in this sort of habitat. A likely example might be a Mallard or Moorhen. If you have an ornamental fish pond you are likely to see a Heron or Kingfisher if you are near enough to other more extensive wetlands. Ponds and other wetlands are also extremely productive habitats and many of our flying insects (including dragonflies and midges) spend the immature part of their lives as aquatic larvae. These invertebrates are eaten by birds, frogs and newts (which are in turn eaten by other birds) so even mostly aerial birds like Swifts and Swallows will benefit from the insect life your wildlife pond produces (a fish pond is much less productive as most of this insect food is eaten by the fish instead). Swifts, Swallows and Martins as well as other birds will benefit from larger ponds and wet areas where they are able to pick up beaks full of mud to build their nests.

Any source of water is likely to be used by birds for bathing and drinking. If space and cost is limited the classic bird bath is worth putting in, but a shallow, low-sided plastic dish an inch or two deep (base trays for flower pots are ideal) and sunk into the ground or even just sitting on the ground could be equally or more attractive. Place a couple of stones in the tray up against the edge so if anything gets into the water that is too small to climb the sides, it is able to get out. As with feeders, keep bird baths and drinking trays clean and if possible collect rain water to fill them rather than using tap water. Birds must bathe their feathers frequently in order to maintain their quality and good condition for insulation and flight purposes.

If you encounter freezing conditions in the winter birds will appreciate the accessible water as much as they would in a drought. If you have a pond don't break the ice as this can damage any liner you have and may harm the residents underwater. Floating a ball on the water can keep a hole open in the ice, or placing a pan of hot water on the ice is a good way of creating a hole without smashing around. If you have a bird bath the easiest thing to do is to empty it each afternoon and refill it in the morning. Most of Europe does not get cold enough for water to freeze during the day so you will provide a

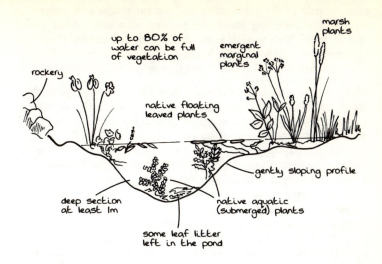

figure 37 good wildlife pond

constant supply of accessible water for your birds. This may be a real lifeline for them.

If you have the space and the means a wildlife pond is possibly the best addition to your garden for attracting wildlife. The ideal would be as large as you can make it, have very gently sloping sides and a variety of different depths with the deepest areas being about 1 metre. At least half the pond should be vegetated with native plant species and be very careful to avoid non-native invasive species (check a good wildlife gardening book or nature conservation organization for advice). In order to see birds drinking and bathing at your pond, leave a section of bank mown short or covered with stones or gravel and allow the rest to establish dense marginal planting.

Birding in your own 'local patch'

Once you have got to know the birds in your own back yard, or while you are still doing it, have a go at finding what birders refer to as a 'local patch'. Birding your local patch is immensely satisfying, likely to improve your knowledge of birds generally more than any other birding activity and, like garden birding, can provide really interesting and useful records of trends in numbers of breeding birds and passing migrants. Many green spaces have been saved from development because the local birders have watched, recorded and can therefore prove the area has high wildlife value and is inappropriate for development.

Many birders find 'local patch' birding more satisfying than other birding activity. You get to know which birds are where, what numbers, which birds are successful breeding one year and not another. During migration your familiarity with the normal collection of birds to be found there will allow you to notice some unusual event immediately. This spring I was fascinated by a 'fall' of migrant Willow Warblers in my local patch (which is also the route I walk the dog every day!). I know from experience that the area supports a few pairs of Willow Warbler every year. They are a fairly common spring migrant to the UK but one morning and for the next ten days, it seemed there was a Willow Warbler singing from every tree and bush. They were absolutely everywhere. I live on the edge of a river valley near the south coast of England and assume these birds had travelled north in large numbers with fair migratory weather. Having found the south coast and being tired from their long journey they had dropped into the first suitable habitat for a break. The sheer number of them was exhilarating. Had I visited the same area on a one-off visit I may have simply thought there were a lot of Willow Warblers around.

To look forward to the returning Nightingale that sings from 'those bushes' most years, to know where the Kingfishers like to sit and dive for fish from, to know there is a family of Peregrines up the valley that rear two young every year almost without fail, except this year. It really is engaging and some of the best, most accessible nature watching you will find. In fact, why restrict your observations of your local area to birds? Watch the dragonflies, butterflies, flowering plants, mammals, reptiles – anything that interests you! So much of the enthusiasm for the natural world and the fieldwork skills you will pick up while birding are readily transferable to other wildlife watching.

One of the UK's most influential naturalists and nature writers, Gilbert White, was an avid 'local patcher'. In fact all his observations were based on the area where he lived! His book, one of the most famous natural history books written by an English man is titled *A Natural History of Selborne* (his 'local patch').

A good local patch should have some or all of the following features:

- It must be local, i.e. it should be close enough to where you live or work to be easily accessible. A local patch that you only get the chance to visit every now and again kind of misses the point.
- Ideally it should be a local 'honey pot' for birds; sites with ponds or other fresh water will provide a likely focus. Ideally it will be an oasis of good habitat, a pocket of the best or most diverse habitat around – this will ensure maximum interest as you will enjoy a good diversity of birds and anything unusual or transient is likely to stop in there. Good examples may include redundant gravel pit complexes, reedbeds, diverse local woodlands, coastal areas, an especially attractive and diverse area of farmland (ideally on a migration route) even town parks and graveyards. The most important thing is that it is attractive to birds and you can get to it easily and often.

You should:

- visit often in all seasons and times of day
- get to know the local common birds, see the detail of their lives
- keep good records of everything you see, including common birds, numbers of birds breeding success, etc. This could become increasingly interesting in years to come as you see trends develop or anomalies arise.

getting out and about

In this chapter you will learn:
- how to get the most out of your birding leisure time
- what to take with you on a birding trip
- how to stay safe in the countryside.

Planning a field trip

Caring for and observing your garden birds can provide a lifetime of satisfaction. Watching your local patch can provide at least that. Gilbert White inspired a generation of naturalists by writing a book about his observations of his local patch. But at some point most of us want to venture further; a trip into the field.

A field trip could, and for many people does, involve travelling overseas, extensive research and expense, possibly hiring a guide and seeing as many birds in a week as you have seen in your life. Or it could be a walk down the road to visit a new site that you think may be promising. A trip could last hours or years, but will always to some degree be an adventure – you can only ever guess at what to expect, you may find a major rarity or you may struggle to find a common bird you had fully expected to see. The natural world is so full of riches to those of us that observe it with enthusiasm that a special trip will always hold some excitement.

Whether you are going to the Arctic or to your nearest nature reserve this section outlines some tips that should help you have an enjoyable trip and avoid some common mistakes.

Where to go?

The first part of planning your trip will always start with the decision of where to go. This may be straightforward, a friend may have recommended a good site and given you all the basic information you need or you may have to do some research yourself. Here are a few sources of information that should help you to choose a good site at a productive time for birds:

- 'Where to Watch' Guides – these books detail all the best places to watch birds, what you should expect to see, where and when. They relate either to your county or may be national or international. An excellent resource.
- A slightly more restricted way that may help you find more birds more easily is to go on an organized guided walk. Most Countryside Departments of County Councils run these; nature conservation organizations such as the RSPB, Wildlife Trusts and the WWT run fairly extensive programmes including tutored courses to aid your learning about wildlife

and led walks around their nature reserves. The WWT runs a year-round programme of events at its sites and these are excellent for getting to see different types of wild animals and plants. Visit www.wwt.org.uk for full events listings, or contact your local Wetland Centre for an events leaflet. As the guides leading the walks may be responsible for managing that site on a daily basis they will have excellent knowledge of where exactly to find different birds, animals and plants. Such familiarity, combined with significant expertise will mean you stand a very good chance of seeing what you set out to see and you won't have to spend long looking for it as your guide will take you straight to the best places. Obviously this cuts down on the sense of achievement you will get from searching things out yourself but these trips make it very enjoyable for you to have good ready-made birdwatching with the minimum of hassle and frustration. If you do go on a led excursion, do respect the leader, even if you are quite expert and think you know better. They have the local knowledge and you could spoil the trip for everyone by scaring wildlife away if you go off ahead instead of following their lead.

- If you join a local birdwatching club they will often organize field events, or you may like to team up with some other friendly members and arrange your own trip. Travel is likely to be cheaper and less tiring with either an organized coach or shared car (assuming everyone pays their share of petrol costs!). One of the best things about going on a trip with some birding friends or club members is that, in a slightly less formal situation than a led walk, you have lots of time to learn from more experienced birders. Birdwatchers are generally a friendly bunch and those who have a little more knowledge and experience will most often be flattered and keen to help when you ask them questions. Nobody knows everything and even those who have been birding for years will ask more knowledgeable friends if they have something to pick up. Some aspects of birding are not so easy to communicate in words, or even with multi-media technology, so knowledgeable and enthusiastic people are probably the best source of learning, especially for tricky things like the jizz of a bird. Often a small group will find more birds than if you are on your own, simply because there are more pairs of eyes and ears.

- Most good maps now list nature reserves indicating them as such. Many actually detail which organization owns and runs them (this could give a clue as to which are best for birds; if the WWT, a Wildlife Trust or the RSPB runs it, it is almost certainly good for birds!). Sites owned and run by local government will be classed as Local Nature Reserves (LNRs), English Nature (now to become Natural England) manages National Nature Reserves (NNRs). These sites often have up-to-date 'sightings' boards helping you to know what to look for, which is half the battle. The WWT usually posts recent sightings on its website, or you can call your local WWT Wetland Centre and ask staff what is around.

- Nature reserves and those places listed in 'Where to Watch' guides are not the only places you will find good birds. A lot of countryside is full of good birds just waiting for you to go and find them. Land management often changes faster than maps and guides can keep up with and the birds to be found there may change too. You could try looking over maps to find good places to find wild birds. This may be less productive at times but because you are using your own skill and knowledge rather than someone else's it could also be extremely satisfying. Good features that may be listed on a map include: mixed woodland, reservoirs and disused gravel pits, coastal areas, town parks, heathland commons, supermarket car parks, rivers and diverse farmland.
- If you are going out alone you may want to look out for places where other birders go. Even though they are strangers you already have a lot in common.

Before you go on your trip it is worth looking up the birds you are hoping to see, checking their identification, voice and habits. This can make identification much easier as you have already limited the range of possibilities to the most likely birds to be found in that habitat and that area. Looking up a few plants that grow in that habitat can add another dimension to your trip and help your broad appreciation of the whole area and how different animals and plants interrelate. In summer look up some dragonflies and butterflies you may hope you see as well. At best this will add value to your trip and, I hope, take you beyond birding into being a naturalist – someone who is fascinated by and studies the entire natural world. At worst it may provide some interest on a day when the birds aren't showing well.

If you don't think you have time for a proper visit, it may well be worth making a brief trip to one of your potentially promising sites to scout around it. Once you are there it may appear quite different from how it was described by the map or guide book, it may be better or worse. New features, or features that were too small to be detailed on the map may be useful, such as small ponds. You could identify the most interesting areas and plan your route for another trip when you have more time.

When you have decided where you want to go, you need to think about when would be the best time to visit. In the section on habitats in Chapter 07, I have gone into timing in more detail. But as a general rule spring and autumn are the most productive times and dawn and dusk are the times of day when you are likely to find the most birds.

Perching birds, or Passerines, are most active and vocal at dawn, so it is worth making the effort to set out early. Dusk is also good but especially in winter when you may catch large numbers of birds coming in to favoured roost spots. You also have the best chance of seeing Owls at dusk. Birds of prey often do not fly until mid-morning (or until the sun has warmed the ground a little; if dawn is four o'clock and the sun is hot, mid-morning may seem rather early) because they rely on thermals created by rising pockets of warmed air. The more you can find out about the behaviour of your target birds before your trip the better.

Of course many species of birds migrate; some birds only visit during the winter and some only during the summer. Some species are present all year round but their numbers are supplemented by lots of their species coming to visit from abroad; their numbers rise and they are easier to find. There is no point looking for a winter visiting duck in June.

Other important things to consider regarding the timing of your trip are where the sun is likely to be relative to where you want to be looking and, if you are visiting a coastal location or tidal river, what are the high tide times. I explain why tide is important in the section on marine and coastal habitats. It is always better and often essential to have the sun beside or behind you when looking at birds. A bird in a tree top, silhouetted against a bright sky (or worse, the sun) is much harder to identify and much less enjoyable to look at. Colours become 'burnt out' against a bright background and the appearance of size can be distorted. Sometimes you will be able to move round to get a better view of the bird you are interested in. Often you will not because on farmland or a nature reserve you may have to keep to access tracks or there may be a physical barrier preventing you from moving around. This could be the case if you were on a riverside, for example. If you can plan your route and timing of your visit so that the sun is at your back for as much time as possible you will enjoy your birding more and probably see more birds. As a general rule, the sun rises in the East and sets in the West; sunrise and sunset times are readily available in diaries or on the internet so you should be able to work out your timing.

Choosing the right clothing

The most important thing to consider when deciding what to wear is that you need to be prepared for changing temperature and conditions, so you should dress with several layers. This allows you to remove a couple when hot and put a couple back on when cold.

Obviously when birding you should dress for the outdoors, but the way you move when birding involves a lot of starting and stopping. For example, you may walk a considerable distance carrying fairly heavy kit including a telescope, tripod, camera and binoculars as well as everything else. Then you stop to look for birds. If you find something good or a promising spot to spend some time you will be standing still, maybe for long periods, and can cool down quite quickly.

I have stated elsewhere in this book how important it is to use your ears as well as your eyes when birding. I would recommend wearing clothes that do not rustle when you walk. Unfortunately a lot of excellent modern waterproof fabrics fall into this category. It is also helpful to wear a hat and not put your hood up; you need to be able to use your ears and a hood will limit your ability to hear the birds around you.

Ultimately, it is more important that you are out there birding and if some rustling waterproofs mean you miss an occasional bird it doesn't really matter that much, but if you have the choice, opt for waterproofs that are quiet when moving. Birdwatching magazines usually have adverts for outdoor clothing that is especially good for wildlife watching, wax jackets have stood the test of time, are tough, weatherproof and fairly quiet. Of course the birds are generally so well tuned into what's going on around them that they'll know you're there regardless of how well dressed you are. The trick, therefore, is to try to present as little apparent threat to them as possible. So, the most important reason to be quiet is so that you don't interfere with your own hearing!

Birds see more ultra-violet (UV) light than humans; they may see colours with a UV 'shine' in the way we do under UV lights in a disco. I have read that clothes are sometimes treated with a colour enhancer that shows up UV even though the colour to us may be quite muted. Some washing detergents also leave a residue which shows up UV. So, as well as wearing muted colours so as not to disturb the birds you are watching, you may also want to wear old, well-worn clothes that do not show UV light well. If you are really serious you could consider wearing clothes that have been washed in a simple detergent with no colour or whitening enhancers.

The most important thing is that you can stay warm and comfortable in any likely weather the day may throw at you. Camouflage gear is not going to make up for poor field skills and I'm sure that a good, patient birder in a bright red jumpsuit will see more birds than a clumsy, noisy and impatient one in forest green.

Theft and personal security

Birdwatching does not pose any greater risk to your personal safety than any walk in the countryside, unless of course you do something silly like pursue that rare bird into an artillery range (the Ministry of Defence own lots of land in the UK and their sites can be excellent for nature conservation). Here are a few tips to help make sure your trip turns out as well as possible, even if things go wrong:

- Whether you have expensive gear or not, sort out what you are going to take either before you leave or stop the car for a few minutes and sort your gear before arriving at the car park. Car parks in rural locations often draw the attention of thieves and you never know who may be watching you put your thousand pound scope or expensive camera gear into the boot of the car when you decide not to take it with you. If you stop and put things away in the boot before you arrive you can leave your car clear of any visible valuables and reduce the chance of theft. Even if you leave something of little real value on show, the cost and inconvenience of repairing a broken window can be greater than the stolen items.
- When doing any outdoor activity, especially if alone, always tell someone where you are going, when you expect to return

and arrange to contact them when you do. If you are lost, hurt or have broken down this can be a valuable last line of defence. If it suits you to plan your route in advance, advise them of this as well.
- Go with someone else if you possibly can.
- Make sure you take some essentials, even if you think you are not going to be out for very long. You may want to stay longer if things are going well and if you get lost or have to navigate your way around an unforeseen obstacle (I have often planned a route to find that what are dry fields in summer have been submerged in water in winter) a trip of a couple of hours can, very occasionally, end up lasting most of the day. So always carry water and food, especially on hot days when it is important to stay hydrated. When the weather is cold sufficient clothing is essential and a hot drink in a thermos flask is always welcome even if you don't find yourself in a minor crisis.
- Make sure you know of the access restrictions relating to the area you are visiting. If the land you are planning to visit is not open access and there is no right of way you must get the landowner's permission prior to your trip.
- Some other really useful things you might take include: plenty of change to use a payphone if necessary or pay for the car park you thought was free; a pocket knife; lens cleaning cloth; sunscreen in the summer; and a change of clean, dry clothes in the car often turn out to be a delightful luxury.
- Because birding is often a stop-start type of activity even the less fit members of the group are unlikely to be left behind, but sometimes you may want to cover more ground or go into more challenging terrain, maybe even mountains, to find certain birds. When in a group you should always stay together and travel at the pace of the slowest member. If any member of the group is uncomfortable about their ability to handle the terrain ahead you should not continue.

Birding etiquette

When birding with others, their observations can be very welcome. I often find myself either birding alone or leading a group. I have one very good birding friend who works in Africa and when he is in the UK I really enjoy going birding with him. It's usually just the two of us and we have similar ability (well, actually, he is such a good birder that he makes me feel like a total novice, but we get on well). I would find it really odd and slightly rude if he saw birds and didn't point them out to me. It would feel like he wasn't sharing. I also admire his ability to see lots of birds as soon as we arrive in the area, leaving me saying, 'Really? Where?' as I gaze at a nondescript speck in the distance. Knowing that he is going to call the birds as he sees them means that if I call a bird first I found it first. I'm not really competitive about birding but it is satisfying to know that I have found some birds on our trips and made a contribution. A very different situation might be leading a group of birdwatchers who are trying to improve their skills or are visiting a site they haven't been to before. The point is, in group situations, calling out a bird when you see it may be very welcome or very unwelcome and everything in between. Even when you are birding with good friends it may be worth establishing your own etiquette as, being your friends, they may tolerate you doing things that are annoying but they don't say anything so as to not hurt your feelings. When you are with a group you don't know so well the best approach is to wait and see what everyone else is doing and take your cue from there.

You will find most birders are friendly, always willing to share their knowledge and perhaps a view of a good bird down their scope if you don't have one, and are an all-round good bunch of people whose relaxed approach to their pastime upsets no one. You are a part of this community and are responsible for playing your part in making sure that watching birds and other wildlife remains an accessible and welcoming pastime for years to come. We all get birds wrong sometimes and there is nothing to be gained by making someone feel silly when they do. We are or were all novices at some point and should expect to be treated kindly and patiently and do the same to others as we gain more knowledge and experience. Competitive birding, listing or twitching, is good fun and a passion for many people, but I find the very common Blackbird more beautiful and fascinating the more I see it. I also like to go to see very rare birds. I enjoy birds. I hope you will always be supportive and generous to others who share your love of birds whether they are on course for the world's biggest list of birds seen or love feeding the ones in their garden.

For more information on birdwatching etiquette see the birdwatcher's code in Chapter 09.

07

different types of birds and how to recognize them

In this chapter you will learn:
- important background information about a few of the more common families of birds.

An overview of some families (groups) of birds

This section provides an overview of some of the most common families of birds. 'Family' is used in the taxonomic sense. It refers to groups of species that are related to each other in sharing common evolutionary ancestors and that therefore have some similarities in their bodies and life strategy (the way they make their way in the world).

Your field guide and other specialist books can provide detailed information on the identification, different plumages and so on of these birds. The purpose of this section is to complement your field guides with some general background to the birds you may see, to nurture your interest in their 'behind the scene' lives as well as how they look and to encourage you to think about the similarities and differences between them. I think it is helpful when learning about any wild plants and animals to start with general principles and then learn specific examples.

A friend and colleague who is an excellent naturalist advised me to learn the families of plants first, rather than just grabbing the nearest plant and working through identification keys (which can be time-consuming and frustrating) to find which species it was. By taking this more systematic approach to learning it is much easier to know where to start when presented with an unfamiliar bird, plant or other animal. It will have certain characteristics that may allow you to place it in a family even though you do not know what it is. It is easier to place a bird as one of 60+ families occurring in the European area than to try to work out which one of over 700 species it is.

Family: *Turdidae* – the Thrushes (and Chats)

There are 330 species of thrush worldwide. They occupy every continent except the Antarctic and are one of the most familiar and beautiful families of birds. Several species do very well from associating closely with man but without being degraded into the ratty character of the Feral Pigeon.

Thrushes tend to be strong, upright, medium-sized birds. The true thrushes are larger; familiar examples being the Blackbird in the UK and Europe and the American Robin in the US. Two similarly common representatives of the 'Chats', Starts and Wheatears, their smaller cousins, are the European Robin and Eastern Blue Bird in the US.

The Robin is Britain's favourite bird. The Robin's breeding range is from the Azores to the Ob River in Russia and from North Norway to the Canary Islands, off the coast of North Africa. They are associated with Christmas for a number of reasons, one being that first British postmen wore red and were known as 'Robins', and this is why Robins are often depicted on Christmas cards carrying a letter in their beak. In folklore Robins have been seen as benevolent animals that should be protected from any harm; Blake wrote, 'a Robin in a cage, puts all heaven in a rage'.

Next time you see a Robin, which will inevitably be soon, have a closer look. You will notice how large their eyes are compared with tits and finches. How sharp and aggressive they are, even to other species. Legend has it that the Robin was trying to remove thorns from Jesus' crucifixion crown and wounded itself, bleeding onto its chest, at the same time being blessed for its kindness and receiving a red breast for ever. However, that red breast has one function – to flash aggressively at rivals: successfully combined with a song duel the Robin will enjoy a peaceful new year without too many fights.

Habitat

As a rule thrushes are birds of woodland, upland, moorland, heathland and forest. Their adaptability has allowed some species to exploit various other habitats as well, but most of us will know them from the created 'woodland edge' habitat of our gardens where the most common species thrive alongside us.

They eat invertebrates and fruit almost exclusively. Two species, the Mistle Thrush in Europe and Townsend's Solitaire in the US are closely linked with the lives of the Mistletoe and Juniper tree respectively; both these birds eat the fruit of the tree and then distribute the indigestible seeds in their faeces.

Thrushes often make a welcome contribution to the keen gardener as they tend to favour eating snails and other garden pests.

Characteristic features

Many thrushes and chats are very clearly sexually dimorphic, others are not. The European Blackbird is black in the male and drab brown in the female and most Chats and Wheatears also differ in appearance between male and female.

Juvenile birds in this family are usually drab and speckled versions of their parents.

Thrushes are strong flyers, usually with a bounding flight, or twisting and turning low through woodland. Larger thrushes characteristically work their way through the woodland floor, noisily tossing leaves from side to side in their hunt for worms and other tasty invertebrates. Smaller birds, including the European Robin and Eastern Blue Bird will hunt from a low perch, jumping down to the ground when they see or hear something interesting.

This is a family of beautiful songsters – some sing all year round (except when in moult) and most have a lovely, loud, fluting song that many will be familiar with way before they ever thought of getting into birdwatching proper.

Seasonal behaviour, distribution and status

Most thrushes are strong migrants, almost all in Europe are. In the UK the best known will be the Redwing and Fieldfare, both winter visitors to the UK. Many species are also resident and some have both resident and migratory populations which overlap depending on where they come from.

For example, European Blackbirds are rather more dynamic than their 'garden bird' nature suggests. Blackbirds are originally birds of woodland and woodland edge. We like our suburban gardens to have lawns, ponds, shrubs and small trees; in fact we like them to be almost woodland edge. We have therefore assisted the Blackbird in becoming one of the most common and widespread birds in Europe. Prior to this massive habitat creation project (the suburban garden) they may have been much less common, but that would mean going back quite a few years. They are certainly expanding their range, having spread significantly north in the last 50 years, especially when breeding in towns. Finland, Switzerland, the Baltic Republics and the Leningrad region have seen big increases over the past 30 years, as has Israel.

And not only is the Blackbird expanding through Europe and beyond, the species is also partially migratory (northern populations highly so), and may be becoming more so as it spreads into northern countries.

Life story and social behaviour

Generally thrushes will be monogamous during the breeding season, and also highly territorial. This may be why they have developed such powerful and complex songs; a sound that we find beautiful but which may not have such a gentle purpose as we think. Of course, they are singing to lure a mate, but they will only get a good mate and rear young successfully if they have a good territory – and that means seeing off the competition!

The Robin's scientific name is *Erithacus rubecula* from the Greek *erithakos*, a solitary bird, *ruber*, Latin for red and *culus*, a diminuitive suffix. Therefore we have a 'little red solitary bird'. Even the most casual observer will be aware that the Robin is solitary and territorially aggressive. Most disputes will be resolved with singing duels but fights do occur with birds flying at each other, batting their opponent with wings and grabbing with feet. Once they have a grip on each other they will start to wrestle, each bird trying to gain a dominant position where he can peck his opponent, usually in the eyes. Damaged eyes are not uncommon in Robins and the pecking is sometimes so brutal it will end in death for the loser. Their songs may be lovely but they are territorial markers and an exhibition of masculine aggression too.

Family: *Paridae* (and *Aegithalidae*) – the Tits, Titmice or Chickadees

These are active little birds, comprising two families. The main family are the 'true' tits and the smaller family is that of the Long-tailed Tits (see Plate 10). There are up to 60 species worldwide with only one of the species of Long-tails occurring in Europe, the rest coming from Central and North America.

They are generally small and compact in body shape and, they have no slender neck as other small birds, in fact their head sits directly on their shoulders. They all have very small, short bills, are very acrobatic, often hanging upside down from small branches while looking for food.

They are charming birds and likely to be the ones you see most on a day-to-day basis.

Long-tailed Tits are very charismatic little birds. Their bodies are almost round and their tail protrudes probably three times the length of their body, giving them a very distinctive shape. In winter they are often encountered moving along in small flocks, busily searching the trees for invertebrates and constantly calling to each other with their 'thrip thrip' contact call. They obviously caught the attention of country folk in the past as there are several evocative old local names for them. Hedge Mumruffin is just one; others include Nimble Tailor, Prinpriddle and Oven Builder (this relates to the shape of the nest they build).

Long-tailed Tits weave domed, almost bottle-shaped nests made from a carpet of moss, lichen, spider webs and feathers. These are quite beautiful and surprisingly strong, the inside is lined with loads of soft feathers and once the female starts incubating she will sit deep in the nest with her long tail folded up above her head, effectively 'closing' the hole at the top of the nest.

Long-tailed Tits are also interesting socially; they are not particularly territorial as pairs and individuals but tend to form clans, typically of 5–20 birds, that you will see moving around in the winter when they are inseparable. The clan hold a territory, averaging around 20 ha, and this is generally defended against neighbours, although sometimes larger groups come together due to food shortages in winter and to achieve greater safety in numbers, possibly some other birds become less territorial under very hard conditions. So, pairs do not hold distinct territories but will establish loose boundaries within the clan territory; sometimes nests will be as close as 20 metres. What disputes there are tend to be about mates rather than individual territories.

Another 'neighbourly' trait of this species is that non-paired birds normally co-operate with a breeding pair (in studies six out of ten pairs do this) and help with feeding the adult female as well as feeding youngsters. These are normally males because as the young birds start to mature the males stay in their parental clan but the females disperse to join other clans.

Habitat

Generally a woodland species, other more specialist species still prefer habitats with tall dense architecture including scrubby wetland and reedbed. These are primarily insectivorous birds that supplement their diets with seeds, especially in cold winter months when invertebrates are not available.

Our most common species are birds of woodland edge, which are therefore at home in our gardens. Most species will come to feeders for peanuts (in fact they are the most common and numerous species at most British peanut feeders) and are often the most likely species to use artificial nest boxes as they would naturally nest in holes in old and dead trees; most nest boxes are designed to mimic this habitat.

Characteristic features

Most sexes of tit at first appear to share the same colours and markings in plumage; closer, more practised observation will reveal subtle differences that enables them to be told apart. Populations move around, especially south during cold winter weather and different 'races' can often be told apart by observing subtle differences in plumage – it can be interesting to know whether the birds you are looking at are resident or immigrant visitors.

Their flight is best adapted for high manoeuvrability over short distances; they have a weak, fluttery, bounding flight when flying from cover but zip about expertly among cover and over short distances.

Tits are very vocal birds, emitting 'fzzzzzz', 'chrrr' and even 'pinging' calls almost constantly. British birders say that if you are in woodland habitat and hear a call you can't place it is almost always a Great Tit, which have lots of different vocalizations and may mimic other species. It is definitely worth getting to know the songs and calls of common tits really well as they are variable and you will hear them so often.

Seasonal behaviour, distribution and status

Tits are mostly resident but some populations may move in cold weather. All except for the more specialist species tend to be abundant and widespread wherever there is suitable habitat and around parks and gardens. They are one of the most easily found groups of birds.

Life story and social behaviour

One of the interesting behavioural traits of this group is the formation of large mixed flocks in winter. When birding in woodland in winter you may spend a while looking for birds, having found very few, when all of a sudden dozens come along at once. These will be mostly a noisy flock of tits, comprising several species and with the odd Treecreeper, wintering Warbler, Woodpecker or Nuthatch in tow.

Winter is a hard time for any small animal as the high surface area to volume ratio of their bodies makes it hard to keep a high enough core temperature to stay alive. Some small birds like tits and Wrens huddle together on cold nights to share warmth; you may find the comfortable cavities provided by your nesting boxes have a more year-round benefit than you first thought.

Although different species of tit live closely alongside each other they are adapted to exploit subtly different niches within the same habitat. Great Tits, Blue Tits and Coal Tits are all very similar, except for differences in plumage and size. Their body proportions and food items are quite similar. Great Tits, weighing in at 18 g, being larger and heavier, seek food in crevices in the bark of tree trunks and stronger inner branches. Blue Tits are a little smaller and can exploit food sources further out on thinner branches. The smallest of them, the Coal Tit, is half the weight of a Great Tit and can be seen acrobatically dangling on the outer twigs, picking insects from the surfaces of leaves.

Family: *Fringillidae* – the Finches

To understand the life of a finch think about seeds. Finches are seed-eating machines. With 128 species worldwide, they are smallish (smaller than 'true' thrushes but larger than most of the tits), tend to be boldly marked, fly and sing strongly.

They include such famous birds as the Canary and the Galapagos Finches, which were studied by Darwin when formulating his ideas about evolution. The adaptations in bill shape and size in Galapagos Finches occur over such a short time and to such an extent that real, evolutionary adaptation can be observed within a human lifetime.

Finches can be grouped into two groups, or sub-families: the Fringillines and Carduelines. The Fringillines are represented by only three species but include Britain's second commonest bird, the Chaffinch. Fringillines feed on the ground, unlike the Carduelines which, although they do sometimes feed from the ground, possess the ability to feed directly on the plants that provide their seed food.

Finches' beaks are highly variable and careful observation can provide clues into the bird's life story. Goldfinches have longer, thinner beaks for reaching into plants like the teasel for smaller seeds, Crossbills have the most highly adapted and odd-looking beak as the tips overlap and cross over, hence the name. The reason for this is that the Crossbill feeds exclusively on pine nuts and uses its beak to lever open the cone, reaching in with its tongue to extract the nut. Young Crossbills cannot feed themselves until their beak has grown long enough to cross over at the end; adult Crossbills use either their right or left foot to hold the cones they are feeding on, depending on whether their beak crosses to the right or left.

Habitat

Finches need seeds so they tend to occur in woodland and hedgerow habitats where there are plenty of seeds and fruits, although they can also do well in farmland and any other habitat where there are seeds. The more specialist they are the more they are closely linked to their food plant; a Crossbill's life revolves around the pine crop, even to the extent that they breed in mid-winter as this is when their food is most abundant.

Characteristic features

Most finches are boldly marked; bold markings can be especially useful when identifying a bird from a fleeting glimpse in flight. Males and females are usually differently marked and can be told apart easily in many species.

Finches tend to be strong flyers, often crossing large open areas with an undulating flight. Many species call in-flight which can make identification straightforward even from a distance if you know what you are listening for.

Typically finches are one of the most vocal groups of birds; some have a simple structure to their songs (Chaffinch), while others are quite complex (Goldfinch).

Seasonal behaviour, distribution and status

Most finches are both resident and migrant, with populations in northern European countries migrating south in large numbers. Some are only seen as winter visitors to the UK or are rare breeders but very numerous as winter visitors.

Life story and social behaviour

If you have a seed feeder try to watch Greenfinches taking a sunflower seed in their beak, splitting it and rolling it round with their tongue to extract the kernel and letting the husk fall away – and on to the next one. Blue Tits will also take sunflower seeds but tend to hold them against the branch in their feet and hammer away at them – not nearly so elegant.

A characteristic unique to the finches is the structure of their bills and skulls. Finches have two grooves in their upper mandible, so when you see them taking a seed neatly into their bill they are slotting it up into one of these grooves. The lower mandible closes onto the seed and splits it while the tongue rolls the kernel away from the husk. No other group of birds can do this and the finches also have strengthened skulls to handle the force that their muscles bring into play when splitting the seed. Different finches have different beak designs, specializing further into specific types of seeds.

The bird most skilled at this, the Hawfinch, *Coccothraustes Coccothraustes* (from the Greek meaning nut cracker) is a good example of a more specialized finch. This is a *big* finch, the biggest in Northwestern Europe. They are so big because they have a big head and bill which is needed to open large nuts. Imagine the power needed to open a cherry stone or, as Mediterranean Hawfinches do, an olive stone. In experiments it was calculated that Hawfinches are applying well over 160 lb of pressure when opening nuts.

Family: *Columbidae* – the Pigeons and Doves

There is no scientific difference between the words pigeon and dove, they are often used interchangeably for the same species in different regions, although pigeon can refer to larger members of the family. The real split with this family is that some are mainly eaters of seeds and grain and others mainly fruit. This leads to some physiological differences between them as their digestive systems are adapted to benefit from one food source rather the other.

There are 309 species of pigeon and dove globally and most of the species from this family occur in the tropics where they are seed eaters. Birders in Northern Europe are more familiar with a few species that are adapted for a life on seed and grain with fruit like ivy berries (a favourite of the Woodpigeon).

The most familiar is the Feral Pigeon, a bird that exploits urban lives very successfully. Like many other species that have made the move into towns and cities, this bird comes from a species primarily adapted for life on cliffs and mountains; buildings simply become artificial versions of these.

The Dove is a powerful symbol for us. In ancient Greece it was a bird of Athena which represented the renewal of life; Noah released it from the Ark for it to return with an olive branch to tell him the floods had ended and therefore God had shown forgiveness; and folklore has it that devils and witches can turn themselves into any animal except a Dove.

Apparently homing pigeons have been used by Genghis Khan and saw considerable use in the First and Second World Wars. I have even read sad reports of Peregrine Falcons being persecuted during the last war because they favour pigeons as a prey item and may have intercepted the messages!

Habitat

Generally these are birds of woodland, coastal cliffs and mountains and, of course, urban habitats. Some will nest in cavities but typically they build a loose nest of twigs, which sometimes falls down during building.

Characteristic features

These are medium-sized birds with a full body shape and relatively small head that bobs as they walk along. They have a short, blunt beak with a fleshy base. Plumage among Feral Pigeons can vary due to selective breeding when they are kept domestically. The sexes are generally similar and juvenile birds look like their parents except for some bold characteristic markings.

Pigeons and doves have a powerful, fast flight with a distinctive 'clipped' wing beat, after a powerful down stroke the wings appear to pause momentarily. Woodpigeons clatter powerfully out of trees when disturbed and the sound of this take-off is quite distinctive. Pigeons may also clap their wings in display flight and perform gliding displays.

Pigeons and doves coo, bubble and wheeze when singing and courting. Most people will be familiar with their song and it is an easy one to mimic. Rhythm and quality of voice can seem only subtly different at first but with only a little practice you will be able to tell species apart. As these birds are often in woodland it is well worth learning their songs and calls to increase your chances of finding them.

Seasonal behaviour, distribution and status

In Britain most species of pigeon are resident (the Turtle dove is a summer visitor), although both summer and winter visitors swell the numbers.

Life story and social behaviour

One of the most striking things about pigeons' biology is that they produce milk for their young, at least when they are very small. This high protein 'crop milk' is created by the sloughing off of cells in the crop and is high in protein and other essential foods. The result is that the young of this family grow quicker than they would otherwise.

The plump look of pigeons and doves is rather misleading. They aren't overweight at all, it is all muscle. These birds are strong flyers, one of the reasons why they have been used for centuries as messenger birds, and the depth of their chests is a reflection of how much muscle is packed away in there. A homing pigeon can happily cruise at 30 mph and reach top speeds of 60 mph. No wonder the Peregrine Falcon has developed a 200 mph dive to catch them!

Family: *Sylviidae* – the Old World Warblers

These little birds are often brown. Sometimes telling them apart can be really tricky especially if you do not know or do not hear their songs or calls. Difficulty in identifying them is further compounded by their secretive nature.

But to call them 'Little Brown Jobs' or LBJs is something of an insult. You may well hear novice birders dismissing them in this way through frustration but you would be missing out on one of the most interesting groups of birds if you were to do the same.

There are about 350 species worldwide, which are found in a very broad range of habitat throughout Europe, Asia and Africa.

I have not described the New World Warblers here for lack of space, but these birds, the *Parulidae*, occur throughout the Americas, from Alaska all the way down to the bottom of South America. I think it is safe to say that they occupy the same ecological position in the Americas as the *Sylviidae* do on the other side of the Atlantic.

Habitat

Although they occur in a very wide range of habitats, from open desert scrub to the dense architecture of reedbeds, they share one thing in common – they like cover.

These are insectivorous birds that also take some fruit, especially to exploit the sugar to build up fat reserves prior to migration.

Characteristic features

Warblers are small, Sparrow-sized birds, generally sexes are similar, although some, like the Blackcap (and other *sylvia* Warblers), are dimorphic. They spend the majority of their time skulking around in cover, picking small insects from the surfaces of plants. They are solitary birds by nature, pairing for the breeding season, although in suitable habitat there may be quite a few in a small area.

There are five main genera occurring in Europe (plus Cettia), so try looking up the examples in your field guide to get an idea of the different types you may come across. Species within the same genera can be tricky to tell apart. Use the examples here to compare and contrast:

1 *Sylvia*, example Whitethroat (see Plate 11)
2 *Acrocephalus*, example Reed Warbler
3 *Locustella*, example Grasshopper Warbler
4 *Hippolais*, example Icterine
5 *Phylloscopus*, example Willow Warbler

Generally flitting about flying low from one area of cover to another, they always seem to disappear really quickly when they reach their selected clump of scrub, like they are diving into it through a hole they've only just seen.

Song is one of the best things about this group of birds. Warblers really can warble! And they do, sometimes all night in the spring. The extent and complexity of their singing is dazzling.

Seasonal behaviour, distribution and status

Being insectivorous birds, many of these species are spring migrants. Interestingly a number of species are present in the UK year round and the range of species that remain is increasing as the climate changes. Even the Reed Warbler, which has always been a spring migrant into the UK, is now staying for the winter in very small numbers and surviving. These events are made more interesting by evidence that these are not the same birds staying year round; the birds in the UK in winter are migrating south from more northern parts of Europe. So, although we see the same species year round, it would appear that they are different birds summer and winter. Climate change seems very real when you watch birds.

Life story and social behaviour

Sedge Warblers have a fascinating life story. When they arrive in the UK in spring they will have made a migration from south of the Sahara. Prior to making this energy-expensive journey they feed exclusively on the reed plum aphid which sucks sugary sap from reeds and thus becomes a very sugary snack itself (you will probably be able to find some of these if you look carefully on reeds in late summer). Sedge Warblers store this extra energy as 'brown' fat – this is different to the fat we have in our bodies and can be metabolized very quickly.

The Sedge Warbler can double its body weight in this way and when it arrives at its migratory destination it is back down to its normal size. These amazing little birds make the journey almost non-stop. It would appear that they do it in two or three big stages with very little rest or food in between; they may complete the journey in just 60 hours.

Not surprisingly for a bird that is so dependent on a particular food source and therefore a specific habitat, the number of adult Sedge Warblers breeding in the UK is directly related to level of rainfall in their wintering countries south of the Sahara (and also the extent of wetlands here in Europe but this factor tends to be the less critical of the two).

The aphid feast in autumn is so important that these birds may make shorter pre-migration journeys from Britain to the Continent if there is not sufficient aphid food here, and then they feed up and set off. They are also thought to be very site specific when breeding, in a similar way to Swallows and Martins, which is not surprising when you think how specific their habitat requirements are.

Family: *Anatidae* – the Ducks, Geese and Swans (wildfowl)

There are 150 species of Wildfowl in the world, encompassing a range of brightly coloured and interesting birds, some of which are small and some huge. One of the most flamboyant plumages to be seen on a bird anywhere on the Eurasian continent is found on the Mandarin duck (see Plate 12). These showy little wood ducks have established themselves in Britain, where they number among our many benign alien species. Native populations are found in China, Japan and surrounding countries. As well as being extraordinary looking, Mandarin ducks have adapted to live in woodland, nesting, as a number of duck species do, in a tree hole. The only problem with this behaviour is that ducks produce precocious young (this means they can look after themselves straight from the egg), who leave the nest at a couple of days old and forage for themselves under Mum's guidance. But at this age the young birds have not developed wings and the ability to fly; so the first use of their webbed feet is not for swimming, but actually as parachutes to help slow their fall from the nest several metres up!

Some of the more plainly marked wildfowl are also strikingly beautiful, and very big. Some of the largest flying birds in the world are swans. And just because they are the biggest flying birds do not think they cannot travel far. The migratory route of Bar-headed geese takes them over the Himalayas, regularly flying at up to 27,000 feet (humans need to use oxygen from about 20,000!).

This group of birds are relatively big, intelligent and have fascinating life stories (Bewick's swans – see Plate 13 – pair for life and 'divorce' is almost unheard of). Because they are birds of open water, they tend to be bright and attractive to look at and easy for birders to find and enjoy. Many of us remember feeding ducks on the local pond as children, this is a great group of birds to start with and can provide unlimited interest for the enthusiastic birder.

Habitat

Pretty much any wetland, coastal and marine habitat, even wet woodland could be occupied by a wildfowl species. They graze grass, dive for plants and invertebrates, chase fish underwater (and catch them) as well as dabbling for plants and seeds.

Characteristic features

Typically medium- to large-sized birds, with webbed feet, relatively long necks and small heads. They have plump, rounded bodies and flat, rounded bills.

Male ducks are usually brightly coloured and/or boldly patterned, except when they moult. As wildfowl moult all of their flight feathers at the same time they are vulnerable to predation and males switch during this time to 'eclipse' plumage, becoming drab like the females. Female ducks and youngsters have drab plumage throughout the year, which can make them much harder to identify than their males (drakes).

Geese and swans tend to look similar in both male and female, although subtle differences can tell them apart.

Being so visually impressive, wildfowl do not tend to be the greatest vocalists in the bird world and even the loud honking most swans and geese produce, although great in volume, could hardly be described as musically accomplished.

Seasonal behaviour, distribution and status

All migratory species of wildfowl are winter visitors to the UK except one, the Garganey. Many species also stay put all year and are resident. Wildfowl are big, bright, social birds that provide a magnificent winter spectacle. If you get into birds, you'll have to get into winter!

Life story and social behaviour

Wildfowl have precocious young, which makes them quite different from other birds that put great effort into raising their helpless babies in the nest. Many wildfowl form lifelong partnerships.

For many years the WWT has been studying the wild Bewick's Swans that come over to winter in the UK from Siberia, tracking the lives of individual birds and their lifelong partnerships. These are remarkable wild birds, making a twice annual 3,500 km journey from Russian tundra to Britain and back again.

Bewicks travel as a family group when they migrate to the UK for the winter and stay in that family group until they are back on their breeding grounds. Courtship begins when the swans are still adolescent. They will still have some grey to their plumage as they are not yet fully mature and their courtship will continue until they are nearly mature. It is thought that the adolescents 'leave the nest' back in Siberia, and then newly formed pairs will spend the summer together and their loyalty to each other will begin, ultimately spending all of their time together. It takes several seasons to form the pairing and then further summers together before breeding. Once a pairing is established they almost always stay together for life, attempting to breed each year, migrating and living together. If one of the pair dies, the remaining swan will normally find another mate but may take up to three years to do so.

Family: *Laridae* – the Gulls (and some of their relatives)

'Seagull' is what most people, who do not realize that there are lots of different types of these intelligent shorebirds, call all gulls collectively. 'Gull' describes a successful, aggressive and underrated group of birds. For the sake of convenience, I will include here *Sternidae*, the Terns, *Stercorariidae*, the Skuas and *Rynchopidae*; the Skimmers. Together they account for 105 species of the birds on earth, and inhabit shoreline and some freshwater.

They are aggressive, they are loud and brash, but they are successful, intelligent and beautiful too. Witnessing the piracy of a Skua (called Jaegers in the US) as it forces another seabird to drop its catch is an exhilarating sight and the grace with which a Herring Gull slips along our coast, looking for food, is impressive.

We can split the gulls into two groups. Firstly, the hooded gulls, including the Black-headed Gull (see Plate 14) and the White-headed Gull – the Herring Gull is a well-known European example – and this group includes most of the larger species.

Secondly, Terns are slimmer and daintier. They fly aerobatically, almost floating, diving to pick fish from the sea with their slim, sharply pointed bills. They include the Arctic Tern which has a migration route literally spanning the globe; it flies from one end of the earth to the other.

Habitat

Coastal, with some freshwater habitats. Some gulls frequent rubbish dumps and travel inland in the summer. Terns eat fish, Gulls eat many things and Skuas eat other birds' food as well as invertebrates.

Characteristic features

Gulls are small- to medium-sized birds. They have long, narrow wings and fly with competent efficiency, often quite aerobatically. They have strong, medium-sized beaks with hooked tips, to a greater or lesser extent depending on what they eat.

As with wildfowl, Gulls are very visual in their aggressive and courtship displays and they have little need for complex vocal abilities. Their voices are loud but simple. They live in open habitats and can see each other some distance away. They also tend to be colonial nesters and anyone who has seen the amount of posturing and body language that goes on at a Gull colony will be in no doubt that these intelligent animals take visual communication very seriously.

Seasonal behaviour, distribution and status

Gulls are generally resident birds and may be very faithful to roost sites. Outside the breeding season they may disperse and wander widely in search of food.

Life story and social behaviour

At the Arundel Wetland Centre our most numerous gull is the Black-headed Gull. The scientific name for a Black-headed Gull is *Larus ridibundus*, the first word meaning a seabird and the second from Latin, *rideo* – 'I laugh', a reference to their call. Interestingly, the Marsh Frog is *Rana ridibunda*, also for its 'laughing' call.

Up until 100 years ago, Black-headed Gull eggs were collected in significant quantities for food and this obviously had the effect of limiting the populations that were accessible to people. This has now stopped and in the 100 years up to 1973 the British population has nearly tripled, and is now facing increasing predation from foxes, hedgehog and mink but remains stable. This species is also showing increasing adaptability and some populations may be true 'landlubbers'; not paying a single visit to the coast but living their whole lives inland.

The most striking thing about these birds, other than their observable behaviour, is their beauty. Adults are the bright, fresh white you expect from gulls and the 'black-head' is actually a dark, chocolate brown mask with white around the eyes and dark, blood-red bill and legs. The shape of the head and neck changes dramatically as the bird goes through its range of body language. Much of a Gull's posturing is related to head and neck position and the mask accentuates this.

All the Terns are stunning to watch. They are migratory seabirds, travelling some 3,000 miles or more in a year and wintering on the west coast of Africa. The Common Tern's scientific name is *Sterna Hirundo*; *hirundo* is from Latin and means Swallow. An often used name for these birds is Sea Swallow because their look and flight is so masterful.

Family: Birds of Prey

Most birds of prey (also called raptors) fall into two families: *Falconidae* (57 species worldwide), the Falcons; and *Accipitridae* (221 species), the Hawks, Buzzards, Eagles, Kites, Harriers and Old World Vultures. The smaller families are the *Pandionidae*, which has just one species, the Osprey, *the Sagittariidae*, which also has one species, the Secretary Bird and then there are the New World Vultures and Condors which belong to the family *Cathartidae*.

Habitat

Birds of prey are everywhere, from desert to woodland and wetlands. Some are residents, not travelling far from the places they were born, while others are spring or winter migrants.

Characteristic features

Probably the most important thing for the beginner birder to become familiar with is the wing shape and style of flight of different groups of raptors. Identifying birds of prey in the air is hard. Falcons have narrower, pointed wings and are generally more aerobatic (though they may not always exhibit this ability); Hawks may be of a similar size but are broader winged with less pointed tips, though when these two groups of birds hold their wings in different positions it can get confusing. Buzzards (see Plate 15), Eagles and other really broad-winged birds look more like a bent scaffolding plank wheeling about gracefully in the air.

In some birds of prey the sexes have different plumage, but because you will usually see these birds in flight this detail will be hard to tell. Juvenile plumages differ more and are worth getting to know. In my experience young, naïve birds sometimes allow quite close approaches and are more likely to be sitting around looking confused about life or making a lot of noise; so they tend to be easily found, especially when recently fledged.

Some species, like the Common Buzzard, exhibit a great deal of variation in their plumage colours. If you know their shape and jizz, you shouldn't have too much of a problem.

Birds of prey have strong legs and feet with large, sharp talons, sharply hooked beaks for tearing flesh and different wing shapes, adapted for different styles of flight – broad is for soaring on thermal air pockets, while narrow is for dashing fast after prey.

Seasonal behaviour, distribution and status

Good sighting of birds of prey is likely at any time of year provided you are at a suitable habitat for your target species. Wetlands in winter can be a good place to see them as they may be attracted by large numbers of prey species.

Life story and social behaviour

In the 1970s Peregrines were rare. During the Second World War about half the English population were killed, as they were a threat to the carrier pigeons used for communication purposes. The real catastrophe for this species, however, has been the use of organo-chlorine chemicals in agriculture. Both Peregrines and Sparrowhawks (see Plate 16) eat small birds that feed on plant material contaminated with these chemicals, thus the chemicals concentrate in the predators' bodies, resulting in disrupted calcium metabolism and an inability to produce viable eggs. In 1963 the successful breeding population of Peregrines was just 16 per cent of that found pre-war. Owing to the phasing out and banning of these chemicals and probably a changing attitude to their persecution, both species are recovering very well at the present time and may reach even higher population levels than ever before.

A book I have describes the Sparrowhawk as a 'Fierce, dashing hawk with rather short rounded wings and long square ended tail'. This is a good description of this able hunter of other birds; it rarely eats anything else. Sparrowhawks normally cover a daily hunting range of about 3 km radius, they prefer closed mixed woodland but with enough open runs under the canopy and along hedges to make their characteristic sneak attack. Typically a bird will fly low and silent, using cover to suddenly appear in the hope of surprising small birds. They fly a run like this of about 50–100 metres before perching in a tree and waiting for a couple of minutes, then off again on another run. They are habitual in the runs they chase, their modus operandi is effectively that of ambush so they tend to stake out sites where prey species congregate and that also provide a discreet approach. Sparrowhawks have very long, slim legs for reaching out and grabbing prey and they are ferocious when in the chase.

If Blue Tits have nightmares about the sudden appearance of the agile Sparrowhawk then Pigeons, Thrushes and other medium-sized birds (apparently even the odd Heron) also have plenty to worry about in the form of the powerful falcon Peregrine falcon dropping out of the sky, high above, at over 200 km per hour. Peregrines hunt out in the open or over water and almost never in among the trees like the Sparrowhawk. Peregrines are heavy-chested birds with strong tapered wings making them easy to recognize as a falcon. They also have a shorter tail compared with the Sparrowhawk who uses its long tail for lots of clever cornering in and around trees. Peregrines are all chest and shoulders for high speed stoops and dives.

Summary

To stop here when there is so much more to say about so many fascinating families of birds seems almost criminal. But there is so much to try to pack into this book and there is enough wonder in the world of wild birds to fill several lifetimes of birdwatching – this book is designed to be an introduction and I hope the few snippets of information above have stirred your interest to know more. There is a wealth of books, scientific papers and material on the internet, don't just use your field guide as an identification tool, use it for learning when you're not out birding. Learn the different families of birds and it will provide you with a really solid foundation for the future, whether starting out on birds in your own area or when you first go abroad.

the habitats of birds

In this chapter you will learn:
- that different groups of birds occur in different habitats and can be specific to those habitats
- tips on fieldcraft for different habitats
- tips on when to visit different habitats
- what equipment to take with you.

Some birds are generalists and tend to turn up in most places. Woodpigeons for example do not just occur in woodland; you can find them in most places in the UK, give or take a few very specific habitats. Then there are many species that occur in habitats that are very common and widespread in our landscape, so common or garden birds tend to be widely distributed because their habitat is widespread. Other assemblages of birds occur in specific habitats that may be harder to access or are less widespread; these birds are highly adapted to life in a particular type of landscape and are found nowhere else.

It may sound like I'm rather stating the obvious but seabirds only occur at sea. Very, very occasionally one or two are blown inland in storm or other freak conditions and of course they have to come to land to nest and lay eggs, but even then they stay as close to the sea as possible, nesting on coastal cliffs or small islands off the coast. They are seabirds – if you want to see them you either have to go out to sea on a boat or get a telescope, go down to the shore and look out to sea. Many of the birds you want to see are adapted to a specific way of life. They have evolved to exploit a certain niche in a certain habitat and this is much of what makes them so interesting. If you want to see them you are going to have to make a trip to their habitat.

Some examples of really attractive, charismatic birds you may want to see include species from more generalist families of birds. Many warblers are specific to a certain habitat: Dartford Warblers really like heathland, Sedge Warblers (as their name suggests) only occur in wetland habitats such as marshes and reedbeds as do Reed Buntings, but to see a Corn Bunting you need to visit some wildlife rich farmland. Pied Flycatchers breed in western oakwoods and Dotterel breed in high mountain areas.

Habitat is crucial for many species of bird and it is one of the most important things you should consider when setting out to find a particular bird or when identifying a bird that is new to you.

Farmland (lowland)

Habitat

The 'countryside' most of us are familiar with is a working landscape totally shaped by the activity of man. It may look green and 'natural' but it is a landscape created totally by commercial objectives.

When talking about habitat we use the term 'climax community', meaning the habitat that would eventually dominate a landscape if any limiting factors were removed. If human activity was removed from our countryside the vast majority of farmed land would return to woodland and wetland within a few decades. Countryside would revert mainly to woodland as ploughing, grazing and the use of chemicals ceased. In the river valley the revetments holding the river back would eventually fail and the floodplain would revert to tidal salt marsh or other wetland.

Thus farmland is not 'natural'. This leads to some sad stories for farmland birds as their fate is in our hands and a change in the way we farm can have (and has had) devastating effects on wildlife. The exciting thing is that where we are in control and can bring about change we have as much opportunity for gain as we do for loss.

Thus farmland is not a natural habitat. The birds you will find there are either adaptable generalists or have adapted from a similar habitat in their recent evolutionary past. Generally birds found on farmland are either birds of woodland edge or open country. Many are resident there all year round and a number of interesting birds are found on farmland when they are passing through on migration or just visiting for a season.

In recent times our ability to produce food from the countryside has become far more efficient. Chemical fertilizers started to be used in the 1930s, effective pesticides shortly after and larger machines have meant the removal of hedgerows as larger fields are more efficient to farm. Sadly a lot of farmland is to the birdwatcher or naturalist a green desert. Crops grow well but little if anything else can survive. The seed bank (seeds from wild plants lying dormant in the soil) has probably been reduced by around 90 per cent on farmland in the last 50 years, so even where wild plants get the chance to grow there are far fewer wild plants waiting in the wings.

It isn't surprising that farmland birds have suffered large declines in number over the past few decades and are the focus of much nature conservation activity. However, farmland is still a great place to go to look for birds, especially at times of year when migrants are passing through.

The worst of the pesticides were banned years ago (for example, DDT) and the birds they affected, especially birds high up the food chain like Sparrowhawks and Peregrine Falcons, have more or less recovered. Organic farming is obviously great for wildlife and grant schemes allow farmers some opportunity to manage their land in a way that provides more opportunity for wildlife without having a negative affect on their business.

An interesting area to give thought to is that of country sports. Hunting, shooting and fishing may not seem a natural ally to nature conservation but on many farms, where game is shot, birds do better than in areas where they are not. The reason for this is simple; where people want to shoot game they must provide good habitat for those birds. In providing features and farming practice that benefits wild game birds the farmer or landowner also provides opportunities for other wildlife. Most game keepers have a healthy respect for predators and wildlife law and wildlife on shooting estates can flourish when it would not if the land was managed purely for food production. Hunting is a threat to many species worldwide and has been the cause of many extinctions. But when carried out in a thoughtful and managed way it can also be very good for wildlife. Don't assume those interested in hunting and shooting do not share your love and respect for nature.

Timing

A visit to farmland can be interesting and produce good birdwatching experiences at any time of year. As with many habitats spring is best and mid-summer is likely to be least productive, although don't let that put you off.

Passing migrants will often drop down on farmland especially if they are birds of open country and where stubble fields or other sources of food are left, fields can hold good numbers of birds in winter.

The time of day you plan for your visit is less crucial than for other habitats.

Specific fieldcraft

Where you go will be limited by footpaths and tracks. The areas likely to hold the most birds are the field edges, so make sure you scan these thoroughly as birds can be well camouflaged against the ground even though they may be on open ground. Check hedgerows and any prominent points like electricity pylons, posts and fences. Birds such as Little Owl, Kestrel, Corn Bunting and Linnet will all regularly be seen sitting up on the top of a fence or hedge.

Any water features such as farm ponds, streams and even animal water troughs are worth staking out, as are agricultural buildings or anywhere food stuffs may be stored or have been spilt. Coastal farmland can be excellent for migrant species at times of the year when they are on the move; birding in this habitat during migration can result in seeing an unusually wide range of species.

Try to cover all the areas you think may be productive, stopping and scanning each one well.

Gear

Always carry a notebook for all your birding.

As much as farmland is open country a telescope is useful if you have one. You are very likely to be looking at birds that are some distance away so binoculars at least are absolutely essential. You may be exposed to the elements and you may be covering a large area so make sure you have clothing to keep you comfortable in any expected weather. Take enough water and food for more than your expected trip, so that if you get lost or find something you want to stay and watch you will be able to do so comfortably.

Take a map to find your way and check access rights.

Tips and preparation

You could be faced with a large area to cover and you must remember that it is a working landscape. It is important that you adhere to the areas and routes that you have a right of way over.

Check a detailed map before you go, make sure you are allowed access to that area and try to locate any features on the map that may be most productive. Look for mixed habitat, for example a mixture of fields and woodland copses, field boundaries, ponds and other water features, higher ground and agricultural buildings if you have access to them.

Target species

- Corn Bunting
- Grey Partridge
- Little Owl
- Skylark
- Linnet

Woodland

Habitat

Unlike farmland, woodland is a natural habitat. Relatively soon after the last Ice Age, Britain was covered in trees. This didn't last long however and today, as with farmland, the vast majority of our woodland is a commercial landscape greatly altered, cleared and created by man. At best you will find what is described as 'semi-natural' woodland in the UK and there is very little of this; two good examples are the Forest of Dean and the New Forest – both areas with rich bird life. Only 10 per cent of Britain's land area is woodland, compared to an average of 25 per cent for the rest of Europe. If you want to see a natural ancient European forest you will need to go as far as Eastern Poland.

Trees are just too valuable and land too sparse for too many for us to have left woodland alone. Added to this is the effect of disease, climate change and acid rain. Having said this, woodland, whether natural, semi-natural or heavily managed, is usually very good for birdwatching and a pleasant place to spend some time.

Woodland in the UK is very diverse, reflecting both subtle differences in geography and also management by man. A few examples of specific woodland habitat in the UK include native pine forest, oak wood, beech wood, alder carr and hedgerow scrub. All support different numbers and mixes of bird species and I find it fascinating that different birds favour different areas just metres apart when sometimes there is no discernable difference to a human.

One of the reasons woods are so good for birds is their architecture. Trees are big, relative to the animals that live in them, and they form a structure that protects, provides food, opportunities for nesting and sufficient diversity for a range of species to thrive in differing ecological niches.

Any trees or woodland will hold interest for the birdwatcher. The best will probably be large and old, with wet areas, ponds and streams, clearings, a diversity of tree species and ages of tree and the more dead wood that is left in the woodland the better. Britain's best woodlands are definitely worth a special visit and details of where they are and what you could expect to find will be listed in local guide books, birding magazines and on internet sites.

Timing

Any time of year is good for woodland, although as with most habitats, mid-summer is not great. Birds are busy rearing their young so they are not terribly conspicuous, the canopy of leaves is dense which prevents you from seeing them and they have more or less stopped singing. If you do find yourself in woodland in mid-summer you might enjoy the butterflies and dragonflies along woodland rides and around ponds more.

The best time to visit is from mid-February to early June. Resident birds will be joined by spring migrants coming to enjoy the long days and rich insect fauna, and birds will be singing.

Dawn and dusk are the best times of day to visit woodland at any time of year.

Specific fieldcraft

Move slowly and quietly, stake out any ponds, boggy areas or streams. Transitional areas, edges of clearings and parts of the wood where different species of tree mix are all worth a little extra attention. It is worth stopping, making yourself comfortable and just sitting very still for a while every now and again in woodland. At dusk, nocturnal animals such as owls and foxes are starting to become active, deer are often on the move and diurnal birds are heading for their roosts. When you sit still and very quiet the 'bubble' of disturbance around you shrinks until it is as if you have become part of the woodland furniture.

It is always important to use your ears when you are birding but perhaps more than any other habitat it is important in woodland. The structure of woodland means that birds are harder (or nearly impossible) to see when there are leaves on the trees. Birds also have trouble seeing each other in this habitat so they have adapted far-carrying and complex songs, which are sung at dawn and dusk when the air is cool and still and sound carries well. In spring woodlands are great places to go birding but you absolutely must be prepared to listen for and learn songs and calls.

In winter many woodland birds travel around in mixed specie flocks, so they are not evenly distributed around the woodland but concentrated into small areas. From your point of view this will mean you may get an 'all or nothing' birding experience. Move quietly around the wood listening out for bird calls. When you do come across a passing flock of birds, stay as still and quiet as you can and watch them move through until they are all gone. Often interesting birds bring up the rear of a flock of mixed tits; there is a good chance Nuthatches, Treecreepers and Lesser Spotted Woodpeckers may be following smaller birds, so do watch carefully to see what is about.

Gear

Always carry a notebook for all your birding.

Telescopes are unlikely to be worth carrying in woodland unless you know there are really good, high vantage points to look out over the forest (such as at Kielder Forest or the Forest of Dean) where you could scan for specialities like Goshawk or Crossbill, or if there are large open areas adjacent to the woodland you are visiting.

Binoculars are essential but the most important bit of kit are your ears. Views may not be clear so getting to know the jizz of woodland birds is very helpful. As with all birding a knowledgeable friend can be an excellent addition to your range of equipment.

Tips and preparation

Get up early (really early – before dawn breaks) and explore woodlands as dawn breaks in April and May. If you only do this once in your life you should make the effort. Witnessing the dawn chorus breaking in woodland is one of the most wonderful experiences in nature. Dawn breaking anywhere is always a joy but the sound and number of birds singing at a spring dawn chorus is spectacular.

Trying to identify individual species with the dawn chorus in full swing is a daunting prospect even if you have a reasonable knowledge of birdsong. I recommend you start early in the year, perhaps as early as mid-January, and get familiar with the few resident songsters that are singing then. By the time all the spring migrants turn up you should find it easier to isolate individual species from the mass of song around you. If you routinely get up and explore your local woodland through the spring, newcomers will stand out and be much easier to pick up one by one.

Learn a few of the most common woodland bird songs before you go out. Blackbird, Blue Tit and Great Tit, Nuthatch, Chiffchaff and Goldcrest should all be found easily with your ears!

If you visit a woodland (especially at dusk) listen out for the alarm calls of song birds, usually Blackbirds. Consistent angry alarm calls will often betray the presence of a Tawny Owl trying to snooze the day away or just becoming active for the night. They may also be in response to the presence of a fox – either way it is well worth taking time to investigate.

Check the local guides to find the best places to go.

Target species

- Wood Warbler (spring visitor – great song)
- Tawny Owl
- Turtle Dove
- Woodcock (a woodland wader! Dusk 'roding' patrols)
- Long-tailed Tit

Towns, parks and gardens (living with man)

Habitat

Man's apparent lack of awareness of his life being inextricably linked to the natural world may lead us to think that everything man does is bad for nature. While we may be the major cause of species extinctions in modern times we also, often inadvertently, do things in our built environment that benefit nature.

The diverse aspects of man's built environment provide many interesting opportunities to see interesting birds. Some birds almost exclusively rely on us and our buildings for nesting sites as they no longer use naturally occurring sites. The Swift is really a tree nesting species, historically using cracks or holes in the tops of tall dead trees to build a nest. Today this is almost unknown (certainly in the UK Swifts only nest on buildings) and the Swift is a bird of our towns and cities.

Other interesting species that are closely associated with our built or crumbling – birds tend to do best in areas we would consider untidy or falling down – environment include:

- Swallows and House Martins
- Black Redstarts
- Barn Owls

- Peregrine Falcons
- Starlings
- And of course Feral Pigeons!

Many of the interesting birds that use our built structures are cliff nesting birds; in parks and gardens it is the birds of woodland edge that do well. The mosaic of trees and bushes created by garden planting suit them well. I have not mentioned your own garden in this section as we have discussed it in detail elsewhere in the book.

Timing

The best thing about birding in manmade habitats is that, by their definition, we tend to spend a lot of time in them going about our daily business. One of the greatest joys of taking up 'birding' is that once your eyes are opened to the wealth and beauty of bird life around you they will never be closed. Birds can be spotted wherever you are: outside your office window, driving along a motorway, walking along a seafront promenade, the gardens of your local bar, looking out of train windows, the list is endless. Birding is great when you make a special trip to a special location but after a while birding is something that you will just do without thinking about it, all the time, everywhere. It connects you to the natural world and it is a joy.

Most of the birds that you may want to look for specifically in the built environment are residents and you can look for them at any time of year. Swifts, Swallows and Martins are summer migrants to this country, Peregrine Falcons are likely to disperse from towns and cities once they have bred and a few notable rarities will turn up in parks, gardens and supermarket car parks every year if you are keen enough to 'twitch' rarities. The rare bird you may well want to make a special effort for is the Waxwing; in winters when there is insufficient food on the continent these birds may turn up in the UK in good numbers. The reason I mention supermarket car parks is that they are usually planted up with berry-bearing shrubs and it is these berries that the Waxwings are after. It is a very striking bird indeed – look it up in your field guide!

Specific fieldcraft

The good thing about manmade habitats is that you can be birding in them all the time. Fieldcraft doesn't really count for much; built habitats tend to be so busy with human activity that the birds should be fairly used to people at close quarters. The areas you visit are also likely to be quite noisy and disturbed, so even if you are quiet someone else may not be, and it isn't worth your effort.

As a general rule the untidier the better when it comes to barns and buildings. Productive areas are those which provide food, water and shelter, so ponds and water features can be good, anywhere with bird feeders, rough ground with teasels and other good seed-producing plants. Graveyards are often excellent for wildife (our local graveyard holds a breeding pair of Black Redstarts), fruit trees, berry-bearing shrubs and allotments are all good features to check out.

A wide range of birds can be seen from the car. Kestrels make use of their hovering ability to drop down on insects and small mammals on motorway verges, in fact it is said that the miles of road verges and railway cuttings form Britain's largest nature reserve.

Gear

Always carry your notebook and pen for all your birding.

A telescope is really too cumbersome and not enough value to bother with (unless you are making a special trip to a specific location to twitch a rarity). Binoculars can be useful but not necessary as you will tend to get good close views of the birds you see. Your eyes, ears, a notebook and a little time are really all you need.

Tips and preparation

Local 'Where to Watch' guides may list any areas that are particularly good but there may be few so good as to get a mention. Best to seek out good features and get to know your local areas. Rare birds will likely be posted on one of the many rare bird alert systems.

Target species

- Great Spotted Woodpecker
- Blue Tit
- Blackbird (so common but so beautiful in both voice and appearance)

- Wren
- Wood Pigeon
- Black Redstart
- Peregrine

Marine and coastal

Habitat

Marine habitats can be broadly broken down into two groups: the open sea and where the sea meets land.

The majority of our planet's surface is covered by the oceans; they are vast and vastly productive. It follows that there are millions of birds that have adapted to exploit the marine resource. The one big issue for seabirds is that of breeding; birds need to build their nests on land, no bird has yet developed the ability to make a nest at sea! For birds that spend most of their lives at sea the need to come to coastal cliffs and islands provide the birder with the best opportunities for seeing them close up, and as most species nest colonially this can be one of the most impressive sights in the birding world. Seabirds have quite specific requirements when it comes to nesting; they need ledges on vertical cliffs (Guillemots), flat tops to isolated rocky islands (Gannets) or cliff-top turf to make a burrow (Puffins) in order to avoid land-based predators. The open ocean provides little in the way of shelter for birds and much in the way of danger (although being out at sea means that seabirds generally do not have to worry about mammal predators and most birds of prey cannot operate over the sea), so there is one primary reason for life on the ocean waves – food. Birds are adapted to exploit most of the small fish and animals to be found in the sea and they may travel long distances in order to follow their food.

The coastal habitats, where sea meets land, are home to some birds that also venture out into the open ocean but are generally home to gulls, waders and wildfowl; the shorebirds. Coastal habitats include sand and shingle beaches and spits, estuary mud flats and rocky shores. Estuaries are especially important in winter when they can provide home for millions of shorebirds. Estuaries are vastly productive ecological systems. A cubic metre of estuarine mud contains enough animal food to be the equivalent of several chocolate bars.

The other coastal habitat you should consider is the diverse, scrubby vegetation that often runs just inland from the coast. This can hold good numbers of birds at any time but can be especially useful if you are on a migration route. Migrating birds coming in off the sea may well be tired and drop in to the first suitable habitat they see (at least for a short while). Good coastal sites can therefore produce more birds than just marine and coastal specialists. In winter many birds that spend the summer inland on freshwater habitats will move to the coast where temperatures may be milder and food more plentiful.

Timing

Sea watching and birding at coastal locations can be good through the whole year. If you want to make a trip to a seabird breeding colony you will need to go in June or July (this is great as these months generally have the least birding activity of the year elsewhere). Most wildfowl are winter visitors to the UK and birds such as Grebes move to the coast in winter.

The most important thing to get right when birding coastal habitats is the tide. At low tide shorebirds are dispersed widely over the distant shore and mud feeding. As the tide comes in birds are pushed up closer inland and their feeding areas are covered up. They gather in dense high tide roosts, so get to your favoured site at high tide or a couple of hours before (depending how much cover there is to hide your presence) and wait for the birds to come up to you. If you get it right you will be looking at large numbers of a range of shorebirds as close as they're going to get.

Also consider the position of the sun when planning your trip. You could get the tide right but find yourself staring into the glare of the sun reflecting off the water in front of you. This is unpleasant to say the least and the chance of you being able to see any birds well is very slim.

If you are going sea watching weather movements are important. Check local guides, other birders and the internet. Find out which weather movements are likely to drive passing seabirds closer to the shore; this is the best time to go sea watching. In spring movements are confined to the first few hours of the day.

Specific fieldcraft

There are several ways of getting to see birds in marine and coastal habitats, depending on whether you are after seabirds or shorebirds. To get good views of a range of seabirds you really need to take a special trip out to sea on a boat. Pelagic trips run from a variety of good locations, you will need to pay for these and book in advance. If you're serious about seeing a good range of seabirds they are well worth the effort but you can still get fantastic views of seabirds without leaving terra firma if you get your timing right.

Check in local guides, with birding clubs, in magazines and on the internet to find good seabird breeding colonies and visit them in June and July when you will get unrivalled close views of these stunning birds in a beautiful setting. Seabirds are not used to having to deal with mammalian predators as they usually manage to avoid them. This means that if you do visit a seabird colony you may be able to get quite close to them. This should usually be in a guided situation, even so one should be extremely careful not to cause unnecessary disturbance to ground nesting birds.

'Sea watching' means you are on shore, at a headland where seabirds will pass relatively close to land (especially if the prevailing weather systems are driving them in that direction). You should really consult local guide books or birders for the best places to go as there won't be many of them. You need to be in a sheltered location – being on the coast can be much more exposed and windy than inland, even on a calm day, and wind whipping in between your eye and your telescope can make your eye water so much you will barely be able to see anything! You will also need to sit and wait for some time so being warm, dry and comfortable is important. You should find an elevated position, but not too high up. You want to be as close to the passing birds as possible but if you are actually at the shoreline you will be looking flat across the sea and even the slightest waves will obscure the birds you are looking for. Remember to look for landbirds at migration times as they arrive. Some amazing sightings can happen this way.

Be very careful not to try to get too close to high tide roosts of shorebirds. They work hard to find enough food to sustain themselves and to use up valuable energy in flight from your disturbance can do them harm. Their activity is dictated by the tide and roosting is their only time to rest. Watch from a hide if there is one but keep your distance if not. Consult other birders if you can.

Gear

Always carry your notebook and pen as for all your birding.

For sea watching and birding on open landscapes such as estuaries a telescope is very useful. Don't be put off visiting high tide shorebird roosts if you only have binoculars but sea watching is really quite a specialist activity compared with birding other areas and because the birds are so far away you really do need to have a telescope for any chance of success.

At seabird colonies birds may provide such close views that you don't need your binoculars a lot of the time.

If going out on a sea watching trip from a boat you will need binoculars but not a telescope. The exception to this is if you go out on a large ship like a long distance ferry or special wildlife cruise where the deck is stable and large enough for you to put a telescope and tripod on it. In the UK one of the popular routes is the Portsmouth to Bilbao ferry; passing through the Bay of Biscay can be very good for whale watching and a telescope here is very useful.

For all marine and coastal trips it is very important that you have sufficient clothing to keep warm and dry and for changing conditions. Any ocean or coastal location is much more exposed than inland and what can seem like a pleasant calm day when you leave your house could turn out to be quite cool and windy by the time you reach the coast. There may not be much cover, especially if you are going out on a boat so sufficient water, sunscreen and a hat are essential pieces of kit, even in overcast conditions.

Tips and preparation

Seabird breeding colonies, trips to and around them make excellent opportunities for bird photography. If you find your interest in birds leading you towards photographing them you should definitely make a special trip in the summer breeding season.

When sea watching the birds you will see are going to be far away and almost always in flight. Take time to familiarize yourself with the illustrations of common seabirds in flight from your field guide before you go and as always take notes when you are watching.

Remember that Waders, Gulls and wildfowl have very different plumages at different ages, at different times of year and the sexes may differ (sexually dimorphic). Don't waste time looking at rare species in your field guide, get to know the most common birds well in all their different plumages. If you know the common birds inside out and back to front when you do come across something less common you will be in no doubt that it is worth a second look. I can't emphasize this enough – learn the common shorebirds in all their different plumages, you will save yourself so much confusion in the longer term and enjoy your birding so much more.

Target species

- Fulmar
- Gannet
- Herring Gull
- Black-headed Gull
- Dunlin (get to know it well in all different plumages; in the UK and most of Europe this is the reference wader, it is one of the commonest coastal waders and provides the benchmark for identifying other waders)
- Redshank
- Common Tern (or any Tern, Sandwich and Little Terns may also be easy to find. Watch their flight, it is so graceful and effortless, almost like they are pieces on a child's mobile bouncing on invisible wires)

Wetlands

Habitat

Wetlands are very diverse and hugely productive systems. They are, as the name suggests, where water meets land. They include ponds, streams, rivers, reedbeds, lakes, marshland, bogs and fens, water meadows and many more. They are ephemeral and dynamic in nature, although for our convenience and commercial gain we tend to strive to control them and keep them as constant as possible. In fact most of the wetlands in the

UK have been drained, polluted or otherwise degraded over the past few centuries. In nature river valleys should be constantly flooded, the river will be changing course all the time, creating meanders and ox bow lakes, reedbed and then wet woodland will establish in less disturbed areas, trees will fall to create woodland ponds – the wetland landscape should be infinitely diverse and ever changing.

Because wetlands are so productive (many of the flying insects you see around you will have spent the early part of their life under fresh water) they are either home to or indirectly support a great number of birds and mammals. Bats are not at all adapted for life in wetlands but they are closely associated to them because they need flying insect prey to survive. In winter wetlands are home to many species of duck, goose and swan and in summer many migrant warblers travel up from Africa to breed in our reedbeds and alongside British rivers and streams.

Wetlands of all types and sizes are good places for the birder, even manmade wetlands such as flooded gravel pits can hold a great deal of bird and wildlife interest.

Timing

Wetlands are worth visiting at different times through the year. As with much other birding the quiet months are June and July when birds are busy staying put and bringing up young, although these are good months for dragonflies (the birder's insect), wildflowers and much other wildlife so don't be put off a visit at any time.

Reedbeds and marshland habitat support numbers of migrant breeding warblers in spring and summer, in winter look out for Water Rail, Bittern and roosts of Reed Bunting. In late summer and autumn look for large pre-migration roosts of birds such as Sand Martins, which can sometimes congregate in their thousands, especially in coastal locations prior to making sea crossings.

Most wildfowl (ducks, geese and swans) are winter visitors to the UK and much of Europe. Geese, some ducks and wild swans (Bewick's and Whooper) will graze wet meadows, diving ducks will favour reservoirs and lagoons, dabbling ducks will be found all over, so cover a range of wetland habitats.

In the spring migrating waders will be passing through en route to arctic and sub-arctic regions to breed and may well stop off in freshwater scrapes (a small area of open mud that is periodically flooded and is rich in invertebrates) and lagoons. Those that fail to breed could be on return migration in July (with main return wader passage in full swing mid to late summer), punctuating the birder's year with some really interesting birds at a time when many are quietly settled and hidden, rearing young.

In wetlands with lots of dense cover and secretive wintering or resident birds, freezing weather in winter often drives them out in more open situations and you are able to get good, prolonged views of species you would only hear at other times. Possibly the best example of this in the UK is the Water Rail. They are generally thought of as skulking, secretive birds but in winter, when they get hungry they can be quite bold and provide good views.

Specific fieldcraft

If you are birding in reedbed it is a very densely vegetated, closed habitat. You should familiarize yourself with the songs and calls of those relatively few common species that are specific to reedbeds. If you can find one, an elevated position is good for viewing across the tops of the reeds, especially for flocks of Bearded Tits and, if you visit at dawn or dusk, the chance of a Bittern moving from roosting to feeding areas. Marsh Harriers could be quietly slipping over the top of the reeds at any time but dawn and dusk are very good as they are for all birds.

In more closed areas of wetlands views may be fleeting and birds may either sit tight or take no notice of you and go about their business in dense reed or scrub cover, so with species that use more sheltered areas you may have to have good knowledge of their jizz and calls (Reed Warblers, Cetti's Warbler, Water Rail and Sedge Warbler). In other more exposed waters' edge parts of the wetland you may get the chance of good views, especially of feeding waders (Common and Green Sandpipers, Redshank, Lapwing, gull species and Kingfisher to name a few).

So, use elevated view points and hides where you can. Use your ears, check prominent perches. Reed Buntings are especially good to locate when they are singing (which seems to be a lot in the spring/summer season), Sedge Warblers and other interesting warblers may use song posts too.

Gear

Notebook and pen.

As with other open habitats telescopes are useful, if not essential, if you want to get close views of waders in exposed freshwater habitats, although you are likely to be closer than in estuarine and other coastal habitats. So many wetlands have been drained for development and agriculture that most of the few remaining that are worth birding in are nature reserves owned and run by nature conservation organizations, so they may well have hides overlooking the most productive spots.

Binoculars are very useful as with most of your birding but I think, especially in spring, your ears will locate most of your birds if you are in closed habitat like reedbed, wet carr woodland or wet scrub.

Obviously wetlands are wet. So as well as your usual considerations for being outdoors you may want to consider that your footwear may need to take you into wetter ground than you anticipated, even in the dry mid- and late summer months when you are setting out in shorts and T-shirt! Also, insects can be annoying and unpleasant in some areas, so it is worth considering insect repellent.

Tips and preparation

Generally wetland sites owned and run by nature conservation organizations are excellent for birding. Some of the best birding sites in the UK, on the East Anglian coast, are wetland sites.

In poor weather birds may use the architecture of wetland plants to take cover from the elements so good weather visits are usually more productive.

Target species

- Reed Bunting
- Water Rail
- Reed Warbler
- Tufted Duck (see Plate 17)
- Kingfisher (of course!)
- Common Sandpiper

Heathland and moorland

Habitat

These are open, uncultivated habitats. They are at great threat from development, afforestation and agriculture, principally overgrazing. They represent some of the 'wildest' areas in Britain and have a collection of attractive and important species associated with them that are found nowhere else. The sand lizard and smooth snake are two of Britain's most endangered animals. The Red-backed Shrike is a bird of this habitat and one of the saddest losses from Britain's breeding birds in recent years.

Heathland and moorland may be lowland or upland, they are characterized by heather or rough, nutrient-poor grassland.

Timing

In these habitats timing is less crucial as many of the species are resident specialists, in situ year round. As always spring is the time of most activity, birds are in full song and sightings of birds like Goshawk are most likely as they display.

For no reason other than the aesthetic beauty of these habitats, an evening visit to heathland is always special, the heather and bracken-dominated landscape glows in the evening sun and later in spring there is always the chance of Nightjar 'churring' as dusk sets in.

Specific fieldcraft

Move slowly, cover the whole area, paying particular attention to any ponds and lower, sheltered areas. Heather provides low, thick cover for the birds that make a home in it and when weather is breezy or inclement they will go where it is cosy and warm – where you can't see them. Sunny, sheltered spots in a gulley or the lee of some trees may be the most productive areas. For the same reason, good, calm weather will prove much more productive.

Check high points as well, especially for singing birds. Tree tops, transitional edges with woodland, fence posts and outcrops are all worth special attention.

Gear

As with other open habitats a telescope is useful here if you have one. Similarly, being open it can be quite exposed and you should dress for a day that could feel colder or sunnier than where you set out from.

Tips and preparation

Heathland and moorland will hold a limited variety of specialist birds so it is fairly easy, and worthwhile, to read up on them before you go. Although the habitat is open, the birds to be found can be quite secretive. Learning the calls of the target birds listed below will greatly enhance your chance of finding them. But do investigate any unfamiliar call, as it will in all likelihood be something interesting.

These are often good habitats for dragonflies and other insects; it is worth spending time watching any pools in summer as there is likely to be a good variety of species available.

Target species

- Meadow Pipit
- Stonechat
- Dartford Warbler
- Buzzard

09

travelling further and codes of behaviour

In this chapter you will learn:
- what to do if you find/go to see a rare bird
- tips about birding abroad
- how to avoid disturbing habitats
- about the Countryside Code
- about birds and the law.

Finding, identifying and reporting rare birds

The BTO (British Trust for Ornithology) has these cautious words for responsible birders:

> Mobile phones, telephone and pager services and the internet mean you can now share your sightings instantly.

If you discover a rare bird, please bear the following in mind:

Consider the potential impact of spreading the news and make an effort to inform the landowner (or, on a nature reserve, the warden) first. Think about whether the site can cope with a large number of visitors and whether sensitive species might be at risk, such as breeding Terns, flocks of wading birds or rare plants. The County Bird Recorder or another experienced birdwatcher can often give good advice.

On private land, always talk to the landowner first. With a little planning, access can often be arranged.

Twitches can raise money for a local reserve, other wildlife project or charity. Consider organizing a voluntary collection at access points to the site.

Rare breeding birds are at risk from egg collectors, and some birds of prey from persecution. If you discover a rare breeding species that you think is vulnerable, contact the RSPB, which has considerable experience in protecting rare breeding birds, and report it to the County Bird Recorder or the Rare Breeding Birds Panel www.rbbp.org.uk. Also, consider telling the landowner – in most cases, this will ensure that the nest is not disturbed accidentally.

- If you have the opportunity to see a rare bird, enjoy it, but don't let your enthusiasm override common sense. In addition to the guidelines above:
- If you visit a twitch to add a rare bird to your list of sightings, park sensibly, follow instructions regarding or relating to access and consider making a donation if requested.
- Don't get too close for a photograph – you'll earn the wrath of everyone else if you flush the bird out of sight.
- Be patient if the viewing is limited, talk quietly and give others a chance to see the bird too.
- Do not enter private areas without permission.
- Birds should never be flushed in important wildlife habitats or where there are other nesting or roosting birds nearby.

Birds should not be flushed more frequently than every two hours nor within two hours of sunrise or sunset, so the bird has chance to feed and rest.

Travelling further afield

There is enough good birding to be found in your local patch to fill a lifetime and it would be sad if you ever stopped enjoying your local, common birds in a quest to build up a bigger and bigger list of 'ticks'. However, the world of birds is wonderfully diverse and seeing birds from around the world, different families and species is a tremendously exciting thing to do.

You have two choices for birding abroad:

1 Go as part of an organized trip. This can be much more expensive than organizing your own trip but you normally get what you pay for, for example, an expert guide, usually with experience of the birds of that region, or even better knowledge of the locality you are visiting. Being part of a group also provides you with far fewer logistical headaches and, if you are visiting a remote region, can make your trip much safer.
2 Researching good places to go and organizing your own trip, on your own if you're brave or ideally with friends, can be a real adventure.

If you choose the first option bird fairs are great places to go to speak to trip organizers and find out what is on offer all in one place. Otherwise, you will find numerous companies running trips on the internet and in the birding press.

If you choose the second option you can also find a great deal of information on the web. There are also likely to be 'where to watch' guides on your chosen area. The birding websites listed in Chapter 06 will get you started. Whichever way you travel abroad bear in mind the cost involved will mean you want to be absolutely certain you get the most out of your experience.

Important guidance for birders

The BTO provide the following guidance for birders in order to treat wild birds with the respect they deserve and prevent them from coming to harm as a result of our being around them.

There is a wealth of information on birds in Britain and internationally on their website www.bto.org.

The Birdwatchers' code

Disturbance can keep birds from their nests, leaving chicks hungry or enabling predators to take eggs or young. During cold weather or when migrants have just made a long flight, repeatedly flushing birds can mean they use up vital energy that they need for feeding. Intentional or reckless disturbance of some species at or near the nest is illegal in Britain.

Whether your particular interest is photography, ringing, sound-recording or birdwatching, remember that the interests of the bird must always come first.

Avoid going too close to birds or disturbing their habitats – if a bird flies away or makes repeated alarm calls, you're too close. And if it leaves, you won't get a good view.

Stay on roads and paths where they exist and avoid disturbing habitat used by birds.

Think about your fieldcraft. Disturbance is not just about going too close – a flock of wading birds on the foreshore can be disturbed from a mile away if you stand on the seawall.

Repeatedly playing a recording of birdsong or calls to encourage a bird to respond can divert a territorial bird from other important duties, such as feeding its young. Never use playback to attract a species during its breeding season. (See 'Birds, habitats and the law', in relation to Schedule 1 species in the UK.)

Be an ambassador for birdwatching

Think about your fieldcraft and behaviour, not just so that you can enjoy your birdwatching, but so others can too.

Respond positively to questions from interested passers-by. They may not be birdwatchers yet, but a good view of a bird or a helpful answer may light a spark of interest. Your enthusiasm could start a lifetime's interest in birds and a greater appreciation of wildlife and its conservation.

Consider using local services, such as pubs, restaurants and petrol stations, and public transport. Raising awareness of the benefits to local communities of trade from visiting birdwatchers may, ultimately, help the birds themselves.

Access and the Countryside Code

In England and Wales, access is to land mapped as mountain, moor, heath and down, and to registered common land. However, local restrictions may be in force, so follow the Countryside Code and plan your visit. In England, the Countryside Code and maps showing areas for public access are online at www.countrysideaccess.gov.uk. In Wales, access maps are at www.ccw.gov.uk/tirgofal and the Countryside Code at www.codcefngwlad.org.uk.

In Scotland, access is available to open country and to field margins of enclosed land to reach open country, provided you act in accordance with the Scottish Access Code – see www.outdooraccess-scotland.com.

Although there is no statutory right of access in Northern Ireland, there is lots of information, including the Country Code, at www.countrysiderecreation.com.

The Countryside Code for England and Wales

There are five sections of The Countryside Code dedicated to helping members of the public respect, protect and enjoy the countryside. Follow the links below for more information.

- Be safe, plan ahead and follow any signs.
- Leave gates and property as you find them.
- Protect plants and animals and take your litter home.
- Keep dogs under close control.
- Consider other people.

Birds and the law

This is an outline of the law as it relates to wild birds in the UK. There are more laws related to hunting and other activity, but here are the basics:

All birds, their nests and eggs are protected by law and it is thus an offence, with certain exceptions (see below), intentionally to:

- kill, injure or take any wild bird
- take, damage or destroy the nest of any wild bird while it is in use or being built (see time for cutting hedges)
- take or destroy the egg of any wild bird
- have in one's possession or control any wild bird (dead or

alive) or any part of a wild bird which has been taken in contravention of the Act or the Protection of Birds Act 1954
- have in one's possession or control any egg or part of an egg which has been taken in contravention to the Act. This includes items taken or killed before the passing of the Act
- have in one's possession or control any live bird of prey of any species in the world (with the exception of vultures and condors) unless it is registered and ringed in accordance with the Secretary of State's regulations
- have in one's possession or control any bird of a species occurring on Schedule 4 of the Act unless registered (and in some cases ringed) in accordance with the Secretary of State's regulations
- disturb any wild bird listed on Schedule 1 while it is nest building, or at a nest containing eggs or young, or disturb the dependent young of such a bird.

In England, Scotland and Wales, it is a criminal offence to disturb, intentionally or recklessly, at or near the nest, a species listed on Schedule 1 of the Wildlife and Countryside Act 1981 (see www.rspb.org.uk for a full list). Disturbance could include playback of songs and calls. The courts can impose fines of up to £5,000 and/or a prison sentence of up to six months for each offence.

In Scotland, disturbance of capercaillie and ruffs at leks is also an offence. It is a criminal offence to disturb intentionally a bird at or near the nest under the Wildlife (Northern Ireland) Order 1985.

The government can, for particular reasons such as scientific study, issue licences to individuals that permit limited disturbance, including monitoring of nests and ringing.

It is a criminal offence to destroy or damage, intentionally or recklessly, a special interest feature of a Site of Special Scientific Interest (SSSI) or to disturb the wildlife for which the site was notified. In England, Wales and Northern Ireland, a fine of up to £20,000 may be imposed by the Magistrates' Court, or an unlimited fine by the Crown Court. In Scotland, the maximum fine on summary conviction is £40,000, or an unlimited fine on conviction or indictment.

If you witness anyone who you suspect may be illegally disturbing or destroying wildlife or habitat, phone the police immediately (ideally, with a six-figure map reference) and report it to the RSPB.

checklist of the birds you have seen

A list of the more common birds you may come across in the UK

Aquatic Warbler	☐	Black-throated Diver	☐
Arctic Skua	☐	Blue Tit	☐
Arctic Tern	☐	Bluethroat	☐
Avocet	☐	Brambling	☐
Barn Owl	☐	Brent Goose	☐
Barnacle Goose	☐	Bullfinch	☐
Barred Warbler	☐	Buzzard	☐
Bar-tailed Godwit	☐	Canada Goose	☐
Bean Goose	☐	Capercaillie	☐
Bearded Tit	☐	Carrion Crow	☐
Bee-eater	☐	Cetti's Warbler	☐
Bewick's Swan	☐	Chaffinch	☐
Bittern	☐	Chiffchaff	☐
Black Grouse	☐	Chough	☐
Black Guillemot	☐	Cirl Bunting	☐
Black Redstart	☐	Coal Tit	☐
Black Tern	☐	Collared Dove	☐
Blackbird	☐	Common Crane	☐
Blackcap	☐	Common Crossbill	☐
Black-headed Gull	☐	Common Gull	☐
Black-necked Grebe	☐	Common Redpoll	☐
Black-tailed Godwit	☐	Common Sandpiper	☐

151 checklist of the birds you have seen

Common Scoter ☐	Great Crested Grebe ☐
Common Tern ☐	Great Grey Shrike ☐
Coot ☐	Great Northern Diver ☐
Cormorant ☐	Great Skua ☐
Corn Bunting ☐	Great Spotted Woodpecker ☐
Corn Crake ☐	Great Tit ☐
Crested Tit ☐	Green Sandpiper ☐
Cuckoo ☐	Green Woodpecker ☐
Curlew ☐	Greenfinch ☐
Curlew Sandpiper ☐	Greenshank ☐
Dartford Warbler ☐	Grey Heron ☐
Dipper ☐	Grey Partridge ☐
Dotterel ☐	Grey Phalarope ☐
Dunlin ☐	Grey Plover ☐
Dunnock ☐	Grey Wagtail ☐
Egyptian Goose ☐	Greylag Goose ☐
Eider ☐	Guillemot ☐
Fieldfare ☐	Hawfinch ☐
Firecrest ☐	Hen Harrier ☐
Fulmar ☐	Herring Gull ☐
Gadwall ☐	Hobby ☐
Gannet ☐	Honey-buzzard ☐
Garden Warbler ☐	Hooded Crow ☐
Garganey ☐	Hoopoe ☐
Glaucous Gull ☐	House Martin ☐
Goldcrest ☐	House Sparrow ☐
Golden Eagle ☐	Iceland Gull ☐
Golden Oriole ☐	Icterine Warbler ☐
Golden Pheasant ☐	Jack Snipe ☐
Golden Plover ☐	Jackdaw ☐
Goldeneye ☐	Jay ☐
Goldfinch ☐	Kestrel ☐
Goosander ☐	Kingfisher ☐
Goshawk ☐	Kittiwake ☐
Grasshopper Warbler ☐	Knot ☐
Great Black-backed Gull ☐	Lady Amherst's Pheasant ☐

checklist of the birds you have seen

- Lapland Bunting ☐
- Lapwing ☐
- Leach's Storm-petrel ☐
- Lesser Black-backed Gull ☐
- Lesser Spotted Woodpecker ☐
- Lesser Whitethroat ☐
- Linnet ☐
- Little Egret ☐
- Little Grebe ☐
- Little Gull ☐
- Little Owl ☐
- Little Ringed Plover ☐
- Little Stint ☐
- Little Tern ☐
- Long-eared Owl ☐
- Long-tailed Duck ☐
- Long-tailed Tit ☐
- Magpie ☐
- Mallard ☐
- Mandarin Duck ☐
- Manx Shearwater ☐
- Marsh Harrier ☐
- Marsh Tit ☐
- Marsh Warbler ☐
- Meadow Pipit ☐
- Mediterranean Gull ☐
- Merlin ☐
- Mistle Thrush ☐
- Montagu's Harrier ☐
- Moorhen ☐
- Mute Swan ☐
- Nightingale ☐
- Nightjar ☐
- Nuthatch ☐
- Ortolan Bunting ☐
- Osprey ☐
- Oystercatcher ☐
- Parrot Crossbill ☐
- Peregrine Falcon ☐
- Pheasant ☐
- Pied Flycatcher ☐
- Pied Wagtail ☐
- Pink-footed Goose ☐
- Pintail ☐
- Pochard ☐
- Ptarmigan ☐
- Puffin ☐
- Purple Sandpiper ☐
- Quail ☐
- Raven ☐
- Razorbill ☐
- Red Grouse ☐
- Red Kite ☐
- Red-backed Shrike ☐
- Red-breasted Merganser ☐
- Red-legged Partridge ☐
- Red-necked Grebe ☐
- Red-necked Phalarope ☐
- Redpoll ☐
- Redshank ☐
- Redstart ☐
- Red-throated Diver ☐
- Redwing ☐
- Reed Bunting ☐
- Reed Warbler ☐
- Ring Ouzel ☐
- Ringed Plover ☐
- Robin
- Rock Dove ☐
- Rock Pipit ☐
- Rook ☐
- Roseate Tern ☐

153 checklist of the birds you have seen

- Rose-ringed Parakeet ☐
- Rough-legged Buzzard ☐
- Ruddy Duck ☐
- Ruff ☐
- Sand Martin ☐
- Sanderling ☐
- Sandwich Tern ☐
- Savi's Warbler ☐
- Scarlet Rosefinch ☐
- Scaup ☐
- Scottish Crossbill ☐
- Sedge Warbler ☐
- Serin ☐
- Shag ☐
- Shelduck ☐
- Shore Lark ☐
- Short-eared Owl ☐
- Shoveler ☐
- Siskin ☐
- Sky Lark ☐
- Slavonian Grebe ☐
- Smew ☐
- Snipe ☐
- Snow Bunting ☐
- Song Thrush ☐
- Sparrowhawk ☐
- Spoonbill ☐
- Spotted Crake ☐
- Spotted Flycatcher ☐
- Spotted Redshank ☐
- Starling ☐
- Stock Dove ☐
- Stonechat ☐
- Stone-curlew ☐
- Storm-petrel ☐
- Swallow ☐
- Swift ☐
- Tawny Owl ☐
- Teal ☐
- Temminck's Stint ☐
- Tree Pipit ☐
- Tree Sparrow ☐
- Treecreeper ☐
- Tufted Duck ☐
- Turnstone ☐
- Turtle Dove ☐
- Twite ☐
- Velvet Scoter ☐
- Water Pipit ☐
- Water Rail ☐
- Waxwing ☐
- Wheatear ☐
- Whimbrel ☐
- Whinchat ☐
- White-fronted Goose ☐
- White-tailed Eagle ☐
- Whitethroat ☐
- Whooper Swan ☐
- Wigeon ☐
- Willow Tit ☐
- Willow Warbler ☐
- Wood Lark ☐
- Wood Pigeon ☐
- Wood Sandpiper ☐
- Wood Warbler ☐
- Woodcock ☐
- Wren ☐
- Wryneck ☐
- Yellow Wagtail ☐
- Yellowhammer ☐

Test yourself

Can you correcty label the topography of this bird? (See page 36 for completed diagram). You can photocopy this and use it to practise identifying topography.

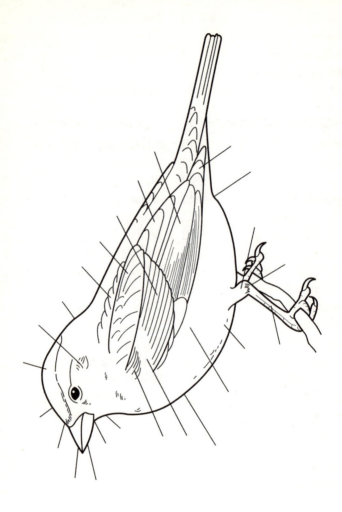

figure 38 topography of bird

Nature conservation organisations specializing in the conservation of wild birds

WWT

The Wildfowl & Wetlands Trust (WWT) is the UK's only specialist wetland conservation charity with a national network of wetland visitor centres. WWT is a world leader in the protection of ducks, geese, swans and flamingos and the wetlands they inhabit.

Headquarters
WWT Slimbridge
Gloucester
GL2 7BT
Tel: 01453 891 900
Fax: 01453 890 827
email: info.slimbridge@wwt.org.uk
Website: www.wwt.org.uk

RSPB (Royal Society for the Protection of Birds)

UK Headquarters
The RSPB
The Lodge
Sandy
Bedfordshire
SG19 2DL
Tel: 01767 680551
Website: http://www.rspb.org.uk/

Northern Ireland Headquarters
The RSPB
Belvoir Park Forest
Belfast
BT8 4QT
Tel: 028 9049 1547
E-mail: rspb.nireland@rspb.org.uk

Wales Headquarters
The RSPB
Sutherland House, Castlebridge
Cowbridge Road East
Cardiff
CF11 9AB
Tel: 02920 353000

Scotland Headquarters
RSPB Scotland
Dunedin House
25 Ravelston Terrace
Edinburgh
EH4 3TP
Tel: 0131 311 6500
E-mail: rspb.scotland@rspb.org.uk

BTO

The British Trust for Ornithology has existed since 1933 as an independent, scientific research trust, investigating the populations, movements and ecology of wild birds in the British Isles. BTO's speciality is the design and implementation of volunteer wild bird surveys. BTO's partnership between a large number of volunteers and a small scientific staff has proved to be a powerful, productive and cost-effective way of monitoring wild birds. BTO volunteer surveys vary in complexity and in the skills required. Even beginners can record the common birds in their own gardens. Other surveys require the identification of all birds heard as well as seen, on a survey plot that may be a few miles from home. Some BTO volunteer nest recorders obtain information of great importance from a single nestbox, others make annual expeditions to remote seabird colonies or hair-raising climbs to treetop-nesting raptors, all on their own initiative. Volunteers can also learn how to catch wild birds harmlessly and mark them with uniquely numbered leg rings, after a period of training with a BTO-licensed ringer operating in their area. This makes a vital contribution to our understanding of how birds' survival rates, breeding success and movements may be changing.

www.bto.org

BOU (British Ornithologists Union)

The British Ornithologists' Union encourages the study of birds in Britain, Europe and worldwide, to understand their biology and aid their conservation.

www.bou.org.uk

British Ornithologists' Club

The British Ornithologists' Club (BOC), one of the oldest (founded 1892) bird organisations in the world, has a website that aims to publish papers on avian systematics, taxonomy and distribution. The site includes a history of the Club, names of past and present office holders, and club rules.

www.boc-online.org

Governmental and International non-governmental organisations

Bird Life International

Bird Life International is a global alliance of conservation organisations working together for the world's birds and people.

www.birdlife.org

WWF

Global conservation, research, environmental advocacy, and restoration organization.

www.panda.org

WWF-UK

WWF conserves endangered species, protects threatened habitats and addresses global threats.

www.wwf.org.uk

Proact

Protest, Alert and Action Contact & Coordination for Eurobirders – A (virtual) place to get together and protest with some effect!

www.proact-campaigns.net

European Centre for Nature Conservation

The European Centre for Nature Conservation (ECNC) was established in 1993 with the purpose of furthering European nature conservation by bridging the gap between science and policy. ECNC has become a renowned expertise centre offering support to the development, review and implementation of European nature conservation policies.

www.ecnc.nl.

RAMSAR

The Convention on Wetlands, signed in Ramsar, Iran, in 1971, is an intergovernmental treaty which provides the framework for national action and international cooperation for the conservation and wise use of wetlands and their resources. There are presently 154 Contracting Parties to the Convention, with 1636 wetland sites, totalling 145.7 million hectares, designated for inclusion in the Ramsar List of Wetlands of International Importance.

www.ramsar.org

Natural England

Natural England is here to conserve and enhance the natural environment for its intrinsic value: the wellbeing and enjoyment of people.

www.naturalengland.org.uk

National Audubon Society

A main bird focused society in the US, the National Audubon Society's mission is to conserve and restore natural ecosystems, focusing on birds and other wildlife for the benefit of humanity and the environment.

www.audubon.org

Environment Agency

The leading public organisation for protecting and improving the environment in England and Wales.

www.environment-agency.gov.uk

Other natural history societies and useful contacts

The Wildlife Trust

The Wildlife Trusts partnership, the UK's leading conservation charity exclusively dedicated to wildlife. The Wildlife Trusts are run as separate County based organisations and are UK leaders in both the management of nature reserves, environmental education and events.

www.wildlifetrusts.org

National Birds of Prey Centre

The centre houses one of the most significant collections of Birds of Prey in the UK, and is involved in the breeding and conservation of many different species.

www.nbpc.co.uk places.

The British Dragonfly Society

Dragonflies, butterflies and moths are excellent further groups of animals to study (obviously plants are worthy of attention too!). July and August can be quiet months for birding, but this is when many of these fascinating insects are most active.

The British Dragonfly Society was formed in 1983 to promote and encourage the study and conservation of dragonflies and their natural habitats especially in the United Kingdom. The BDS is a registered charity.

Membership of the British Dragonfly Society is one effective way of helping to conserve these interesting insects. If you would like join the Society please contact the Membership Secretary.

BDS Membership Office
c/o The Phoenix Centre
Station Road
Bordon
Hants
GU35 0LR
email: belinda@broadwaypark.freeserve.co.uk
www.dragonflysoc.org.uk

Butterfly Conservation

www.butterfly-conservation.org

Plantlife International

The only charity in the world working solely for the conservation of wild plants and fungi.

www.plantlife.org.uk

Certificate of Higher Education in Ornithology, University of Birmingham

This unique part-time programme is designed to bring bird-watchers up to date with their understanding of bird life. What birds are, their origins, evolution and classification, where and how they spend their lives and the myriad of ways in which birds are adapted to their unique lifestyles; these are just some of the important areas in which fascinating new information and ideas have been produced. This programme will provide an avenue if you wish to become involved in local and national surveys and research projects – to help you make the transition from bird-watcher to amateur ornithologist. It is organised with the collaboration of the British Trust for Ornithology.

http://www.biosciences.bham.ac.uk/tpd/ornithology.htm

This list is intended to provide a quick start reference to some of the organisations that may interest the keen birder. There is not space to list them all. Two notable omissions are those of County based Ornithological Societies, many of which are active in carrying out excellent work and organising events. Similarly there are many County based Natural History Societies for more general interest in wildlife. Nature Conservation organisations like the RSPB, Wildlife trusts and WWF will also have local member's groups and County Council Countryside Departments may organise local events.

Useful suppliers

General links to everything birding related
www.fatbirder.com
www.surfbirds.com
www.birdguides.com
www.fatbirder.com
www.worldtwitch.com
www.birdersworld.com

Binoculars, telescopes and other optics
In Focus
www.at-infocus.co.uk

Warehouse Express
www.warehouseexpress.com

Bird food and bird care products
Jacobi Jayne at www.jacobijayne.com
WWT and RSPB shops and websites

Wildlife holidays
www.naturetrek.co.uk
www.travel-quest.co.uk
www.earthwatch.org

Further reading

Barnes, S. (2005) *A Bad Birdwatcher's Companion: 50 Intimate Portraits of Britain's Best Loved Birds*, London: Short Books

Barnes, S. (2004) *How to Be a Bad Birdwatcher*, London: Short Books

Cocker, M. and Mabey, R. (2005) *Birds Britannica*, London: Chatto and Windus

Grant, P.J., Mullarney, K., Svensson, L, Zetterstrom, D (2001) *Collins Bird Guide: The Most Complete Guide to the Birds of Britain and Europe*, London: Collins

Holden, P. and Cleeves, T. (2006) *RSPB Handbook of British Birds (Ornithology)*, London: Christopher Helm Publishers Ltd

Oddie, B. (1998) *Bill Oddie's Little Black Bird Book*, London: Robson Books Ltd

Ostling, B. and Ullman, M. (2006) *Life on the Wing: Remarkable Birds and Their Extraordinary Lives*, London: Collins

Rhodes, R. (2004) *John James Audubon: The Making of an American*, New York: Alfred A. Knopf

Sample, G. (1996) *Collins Field Guide: Bird Songs and Calls of Britain and Northern Europe*, London: Collins

Sample, G. (2000) *Garden Bird Songs and Calls*, London: Collins

Tait, M. (2005) *The Birdwatcher's Companion (A Think Book)*, London: Robson Books Ltd

DVD: *David Attenborough's Life of Birds* (1998), London: BBC

index

Aegithalidae family **105–8**
ambassadors for birdwatching **148–9**
Anatidae family **115–17**
archeopterix **17**
arctic terns **8–9**

barn owls **27, 84, 131**
beaks **16–20, 21**
berries **79**
Bewick's swans **27, 116–17**
binoculars **56–63, 127, 131, 133, 137**
    accessories **63**
    buying **58–63**
    using **57–8**
birders **2**
birds of prey **18, 23, 96, 119–21, 144**
birdwatchers' code **148**
bitterns **139**
black redstarts **134**
black-headed gulls **118–19, 138**
blackbirds **26, 30, 34, 100, 102–3, 104–5, 130, 131, 133**
blackcaps **113**
blue tits **28, 30, 33, 44, 108, 110, 121, 130, 133**
Bond, James **3–4**
breeding **44**
BTO (British Trust for Ornithology) **3, 44, 145, 157**
    birdwatchers' code **148**
buzzards **119, 120, 143**

calls *see* songs and calls
canaries **108**
Carduelines **108–9**
cats **77–8**
celebrity birdwatchers **3–4**
chaffinches **33, 109**
chats **103, 104**
chiffchaffs **27, 50, 130**
climax community **125**
clothing for birdwatching **63–4, 97–8, 141**
clubs **94**
coal tits **32–3, 108**
coastal habitats **127, 134–8**
Columbidae family **110–12**
compost heaps **80**
condors **119**
corn buntings **124, 126, 127**
Countryside Code **149**
crossbills **109, 130**
cuckoos **22, 27**

Dartford warblers **27, 124, 143**
digestion **20–1**
doves **111, 112, 131**
drawing birds **37–40**
ducks **115–17, 139**
dunlins **138**

eggs **21, 150**
etiquette **99–100**
evolution of birds **9–10, 18–19**

falcons **111, 112, 119, 120**

farmland habitats **124–7**
fat balls **74–5**
feathers **9–14**
feeders **73–7**
   materials **87**
   siting **70–2, 76–7**
feral pigeons **103, 111, 132**
field guides **31, 32–3, 47, 53–6, 102**
field trips **93–100**
   clothing for **97–8**
   etiquette on **99–100**
   theft and personal security **98–9**
   timing of **96–7**
   where to go **93–4**
fieldfares **23, 104**
finches **20, 75, 76, 108–10**
fishing **126**
flycatchers **27, 44, 124**
food **70, 72–6**
   and digestion **20–1**
   natural food sources **79–80**
Fringillidae family **108–10**
fulmars **138**

Galapagos finches **108**
gamekeepers **126**
gannets **8–9, 134, 138**
gardens
   birds commonly seen in **30**
   wildlife **70–2, 80, 88–9**
garganeys **116**
geese **115, 116, 139**
goldcrests **18, 34, 130**
goldfinches **76, 109**
goshawks **130, 142**
grasshopper warblers **113**
great spotted woodpeckers **34, 133**
great tits **28, 45, 49, 107, 108, 130**
greenfinches **18, 30, 33, 110**
grey partridges **21, 127**
guillemots **134**
gulls **13, 35, 117–19, 138**

habitats **123–43**
   farmland **124–7**
   heathland and moorland **142–3**
   marine and coastal **134–8**
   wetlands **138–41**
   woodland **128–31**

harriers **119**
hawfinches **110**
hawks **118**
heathland habitats **142–3**
herbicides **80**
herons **88, 121**
herring gulls **13, 138**
house sparrow nest boxes **83–4**
Hughes, Ted **33**
humming birds **9, 21**
hunting **126**

icterines **113**
identifying birds **26–51**
   by songs and calls **46–8**
   developing observation skills **29–37**
   drawings **37–40**
   in flight **51**
   from a fleeting glimpse **50–1**
   out of doors **41–3**
insectivorous birds **73, 74–5**
internet sites **67**

jack snipes **34**
jays **73**

kestrels **126**
kingfishers **14, 34, 88, 90, 140, 141**
kites **119**

lapwings **140**
Laridae family **117–19**
law relating to birds **150–1**
Linnaeus, Carl **28**
linnets **126, 127**
local patch birding **89–91**
long-tailed tits **105–6, 131**

mallards **88**
Mandarin ducks **115**
marine habitats **134–8**
martins **22, 81, 82, 83, 88, 131, 139**
meadow pipits **35, 143**
meadows **80**
migrating birds **22–4, 35, 96**
   and local patch birding **90**
   seabirds **23, 135**
   songs and calls **50**

moorhens **88**
moorland habitats **142–3**
moulting feathers **13–14**
mute swans **16–17**

naming birds **26–8**
nature reserves **94–5**
nest boxes **70, 77, 80–7**
   cups **82–3**
   house sparrow **83–4**
   materials **87**
   tree creepers **85, 86–7**
   tree hole **81–2, 84–5**
   wren house **86**
nests **21**
Niger seed **76**
nightingales **90**
nightjars **142**
note-taking **30–6**
notebooks **53**
nuthatches **73, 82, 85, 108, 130**

Oddie, Bill **3**
ospreys **119**
outdoor observation **41–3**
   see also habitats
owls **96, 126, 131**
   little **126, 127**
   nesting boxes **81, 84–5**
oystercatchers **22**

Pallas's warbler **135**
Paridae family **105–8**
partridges **21, 127**
passerines (perching birds) **45, 96**
peanut feeders **70–2, 73, 75**
penguins **8**
perching birds (passerines) **45, 96**
peregrine falcons **111, 112, 120, 125, 132**
photographing birds **68**
pied flycatchers **124**
pigeons **30, 103, 111–12, 121, 132**
pintails **115**
plants
   natural food sources **79–80**
   wildlife ponds **89**
ponds **88–9**
puffins **134**

rare birds **144–5**
rats **79**
reasons for birdwatching **5–6**
red-backed shrikes **142**
redshanks **138, 140**
redwings **104**
reed buntings **50, 124, 139, 140, 141**
reed warblers **22, 47, 50, 113, 114, 140, 141**
respiratory system **15, 16**
robins **30, 103, 105**
Rockhopper Penguins **8**
RSPB (Royal Society for the Protection of Birds) **3, 93, 145, 156**
ruddy ducks **21**

sand martins **139**
sandpipers **140, 141**
sea ducks **115**
seabirds **23, 124, 134–8**
seagulls **117**
security on field trips **98–9**
sedge warblers **8, 22, 114–15, 124, 140**
seed-eating birds **73, 75–6**
shelter for birds **70, 80–7**
shooting **126**
shoveller **18**
skeletal structure **14–15**
skylarks **127**
snipes **27, 34**
songs and calls **43–50**
   listening outdoors **49–50**
   recordings of **48–9**
   starlings **85**
sparrowhawks **76–7, 120–1, 125**
sparrows **82**
   house sparrow nest boxes **83–4**
squirrels **78, 87**
SSSIs (Sites of Special Scientific Interest) **151**
starlings **79, 85, 132**
stonechats **143**
swallows **22, 33, 35, 81, 83, 88, 131**
swans **8, 16–17, 27, 115, 116, 139**
   Bewick's **27, 116–17**
swifts **22, 33–4, 81, 82–3, 88**

Sylviidae family **112–15**
syrinx **45–6**

tawny owls **131**
teeth and beaks **16–20, 21**
telescopes **64–7, 127, 130, 137, 143**
terns **117, 119, 138**
theft on field trips **98–9**
thrushes **45, 56, 102–5, 121**
tits **73, 75, 85, 105–8**
    blue **28, 30, 33, 44, 108, 110, 121, 130, 133**
    great **28, 45, 49, 107, 108, 130**
    long-tailed **105–6, 131**
topography **36**
town parks and gardens **131–4**
tree hole nesting boxes
    large **84–5**
    small **81–2**
tree pipits **35**
tree sparrows **82**
treecreepers **108**
    nest boxes **85, 86–7**
trips abroad **146**
tufted ducks **141**
Turdidae family **102–5**
twitching **2**

vultures **119**

waders **138, 139–40, 141**
warblers **27, 28, 45, 47, 108, 112–15, 124, 131**
    Dartford **27, 124, 143**
    reed **22, 47, 50, 113, 114, 140, 141**
    sedge **8, 22, 114–15, 124, 140**
water
    wetland habitats **138–41**
    wildlife ponds **88–9**
water rails **139, 140, 141**
waxwings **23**
wetlands **138–41**
White, Gilbert **90, 93**
whitethroats **113**
Whooper Swans **8**
wigeons **115**
wildfowl **115–17, 138, 139**
wildlife gardens **70–2, 80, 88–9**

willow warblers **50, 90, 113**
wings **20–1**
wood larks **27**
wood pigeons **30, 112, 124, 134**
woodcocks **131**
woodland habitats **128–31**
woodpeckers **34, 73, 87, 108, 133**
    nest boxes for **84–5**
wrens **86, 108, 134**
WWT (Wildfowl and Wetlands Trust) **3, 28**
    Arundel Wetland Centre **50, 118**
    courses **93–4**
    nature reserves **95**

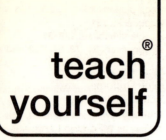

teach yourself: the range

From Advanced Sudoku to Zulu, you'll find everything you need in the **teach yourself** range, in books, on CD and on DVD.

Visit **www.teachyourself.co.uk** for more details.

Advanced Sudoku and Kakuro
Afrikaans
Alexander Technique
Algebra
Ancient Greek
Applied Psychology
Arabic
Aromatherapy
Art History
Astrology
Astronomy
AutoCAD 2004
AutoCAD 2007
Ayurveda
Baby Massage and Yoga
Baby Signing
Baby Sleep
Bach Flower Remedies
Backgammon
Ballroom Dancing
Basic Accounting
Basic Computer Skills
Basic Mathematics
Beauty
Beekeeping
Beginner's Arabic Script
Beginner's Chinese Script
Beginner's Dutch
Beginner's French
Beginner's German
Beginner's Greek
Beginner's Greek Script
Beginner's Hindi
Beginner's Italian
Beginner's Japanese
Beginner's Japanese Script
Beginner's Latin
Beginner's Mandarin Chinese
Beginner's Portuguese
Beginner's Russian
Beginner's Russian Script
Beginner's Spanish
Beginner's Turkish
Beginner's Urdu Script
Bengali
Better Bridge
Better Chess
Better Driving
Better Handwriting
Biblical Hebrew
Biology
Birdwatching
Blogging
Body Language
Book Keeping
Brazilian Portuguese

teach yourself: the range

- Bridge
- British Empire, The
- British Monarchy from Henry VIII, The
- Buddhism
- Bulgarian
- Business Chinese
- Business French
- Business Japanese
- Business Plans
- Business Spanish
- Business Studies
- Buying a Home in France
- Buying a Home in Italy
- Buying a Home in Portugal
- Buying a Home in Spain
- C++
- Calculus
- Calligraphy
- Cantonese
- Car Buying and Maintenance
- Card Games
- Catalan
- Chess
- Chi Kung
- Chinese Medicine
- Christianity
- Classical Music
- Coaching
- Cold War, The
- Collecting
- Computing for the Over 50s
- Consulting
- Copywriting
- Correct English
- Counselling
- Creative Writing
- Cricket
- Croatian
- Crystal Healing
- CVs
- Czech
- Danish
- Decluttering
- Desktop Publishing
- Detox
- Digital Home Movie Making
- Digital Photography
- Dog Training
- Drawing
- Dream Interpretation
- Dutch
- Dutch Conversation
- Dutch Dictionary
- Dutch Grammar
- Eastern Philosophy
- Electronics
- English as a Foreign Language
- English for International Business
- English Grammar
- English Grammar as a Foreign Language
- English Vocabulary
- Entrepreneurship
- Estonian
- Ethics
- Excel 2003
- Feng Shui
- Film Making
- Film Studies
- Finance for Non-Financial Managers
- Finnish
- First World War, The
- Fitness
- Flash 8
- Flash MX
- Flexible Working
- Flirting
- Flower Arranging
- Franchising
- French
- French Conversation
- French Dictionary
- French Grammar
- French Phrasebook
- French Starter Kit
- French Verbs
- French Vocabulary
- Freud
- Gaelic

teach yourself: the range

Gardening
Genetics
Geology
German
German Conversation
German Grammar
German Phrasebook
German Verbs
German Vocabulary
Globalization
Go
Golf
Good Study Skills
Great Sex
Greek
Greek Conversation
Greek Phrasebook
Growing Your Business
Guitar
Gulf Arabic
Hand Reflexology
Hausa
Herbal Medicine
Hieroglyphics
Hindi
Hindi Conversation
Hinduism
History of Ireland, The
Home PC Maintenance and Networking
How to DJ
How to Run a Marathon
How to Win at Casino Games
How to Win at Horse Racing
How to Win at Online Gambling
How to Win at Poker
How to Write a Blockbuster
Human Anatomy & Physiology
Hungarian
Icelandic
Improve Your French
Improve Your German
Improve Your Italian
Improve Your Spanish
Improving Your Employability
Indian Head Massage
Indonesian
Instant French
Instant German
Instant Greek
Instant Italian
Instant Japanese
Instant Portuguese
Instant Russian
Instant Spanish
Internet, The
Irish
Irish Conversation
Irish Grammar
Islam
Italian
Italian Conversation
Italian Grammar
Italian Phrasebook
Italian Starter Kit
Italian Verbs
Italian Vocabulary
Japanese
Japanese Conversation
Java
JavaScript
Jazz
Jewellery Making
Judaism
Jung
Kama Sutra, The
Keeping Aquarium Fish
Keeping Pigs
Keeping Poultry
Keeping a Rabbit
Knitting
Korean
Latin
Latin American Spanish
Latin Dictionary
Latin Grammar
Latvian
Letter Writing Skills
Life at 50: For Men
Life at 50: For Women

- Life Coaching
- Linguistics
- LINUX
- Lithuanian
- Magic
- Mahjong
- Malay
- Managing Stress
- Managing Your Own Career
- Mandarin Chinese
- Mandarin Chinese Conversation
- Marketing
- Marx
- Massage
- Mathematics
- Meditation
- Middle East Since 1945, The
- Modern China
- Modern Hebrew
- Modern Persian
- Mosaics
- Music Theory
- Mussolini's Italy
- Nazi Germany
- Negotiating
- Nepali
- New Testament Greek
- NLP
- Norwegian
- Norwegian Conversation
- Old English
- One-Day French
- One-Day French – the DVD
- One-Day German
- One-Day Greek
- One-Day Italian
- One-Day Portuguese
- One-Day Spanish
- One-Day Spanish – the DVD
- Origami
- Owning a Cat
- Owning a Horse
- Panjabi
- PC Networking for Small Businesses
- Personal Safety and Self Defence
- Philosophy
- Philosophy of Mind
- Philosophy of Religion
- Photography
- Photoshop
- PHP with MySQL
- Physics
- Piano
- Pilates
- Planning Your Wedding
- Polish
- Polish Conversation
- Politics
- Portuguese
- Portuguese Conversation
- Portuguese Grammar
- Portuguese Phrasebook
- Postmodernism
- Pottery
- PowerPoint 2003
- PR
- Project Management
- Psychology
- Quick Fix French Grammar
- Quick Fix German Grammar
- Quick Fix Italian Grammar
- Quick Fix Spanish Grammar
- Quick Fix: Access 2002
- Quick Fix: Excel 2000
- Quick Fix: Excel 2002
- Quick Fix: HTML
- Quick Fix: Windows XP
- Quick Fix: Word
- Quilting
- Recruitment
- Reflexology
- Reiki
- Relaxation
- Retaining Staff
- Romanian
- Running Your Own Business
- Russian
- Russian Conversation

teach yourself: the range

teach yourself: the range

Russian Grammar
Sage Line 50
Sanskrit
Screenwriting
Second World War, The
Serbian
Setting Up a Small Business
Shorthand Pitman 2000
Sikhism
Singing
Slovene
Small Business Accounting
Small Business Health Check
Songwriting
Spanish
Spanish Conversation
Spanish Dictionary
Spanish Grammar
Spanish Phrasebook
Spanish Starter Kit
Spanish Verbs
Spanish Vocabulary
Speaking On Special Occasions
Speed Reading
Stalin's Russia
Stand Up Comedy
Statistics
Stop Smoking
Sudoku
Swahili
Swahili Dictionary
Swedish
Swedish Conversation
Tagalog
Tai Chi
Tantric Sex
Tap Dancing
Teaching English as a Foreign Language
Teams & Team Working
Thai
Theatre
Time Management
Tracing Your Family History
Training
Travel Writing
Trigonometry
Turkish
Turkish Conversation
Twentieth Century USA
Typing
Ukrainian
Understanding Tax for Small Businesses
Understanding Terrorism
Urdu
Vietnamese
Visual Basic
Volcanoes
Watercolour Painting
Weight Control through Diet & Exercise
Welsh
Welsh Dictionary
Welsh Grammar
Wills & Probate
Windows XP
Wine Tasting
Winning at Job Interviews
Word 2003
World Cultures: China
World Cultures: England
World Cultures: Germany
World Cultures: Italy
World Cultures: Japan
World Cultures: Portugal
World Cultures: Russia
World Cultures: Spain
World Cultures: Wales
World Faiths
Writing Crime Fiction
Writing for Children
Writing for Magazines
Writing a Novel
Writing Poetry
Xhosa
Yiddish
Yoga
Zen
Zulu

teach yourself	**keeping aquarium fish** dick mills

- Are you interested in keeping aquarium fish?
- Do you know about the different species?
- Do you need help feeding and caring for your fish?

If you have just started, or are planning, to keep fish in a tank. **Keeping Aquarium Fish** will give you everything you need to ensure they are happy and healthy. It gives step-by-step instructions on what species you should choose, which equipment you'll need and what the daily needs of feeding and maintenance are. It has lots of trouble-shooting sections and helpful hints, and even covers breeding and caring for rarer fish.

Dick Mills is a writer and dedicated fish-keeper who has written over a dozen very successful books on keeping fish for owners of all ages and abilities.

teach yourself	**keeping pigs** tony york

- Do you want to know which breed is right for you?
- Would you like advice on housing and equipment?
- Do you want guidelines on how to spot disease or illness?

If you are already a pig-keeper or perhaps a would-be 'hobby farmer' keep to experience the 'good life', **Keeping Pigs** is for you. It will give you everything you need to keep happy and healthy pigs, from practical instructions on which equipment you'll need, to information on feeding and maintenance and guidelines on meat production. It also has lots of useful resources, including a gestation calendar, and plenty of helpful contacts.

Tony York is a pig-farmer whose courses on pig-keeping have attracted people from across the UK for over 15 years.

| teach yourself | **owning a horse**
carolyn henderson |

- Do you want to know how to buy a horse?
- Would you like practical advice on grooming?
- Would you like to find out about horse psychology?

Owning a Horse is aimed at all those interested in buying and keeping their own horse, whether at home or in a yard. It covers not only day-to-day care from tack to feeding, but also explains costs, which breed to choose, and all the formalities of buying and insuring. Authoritative yet readable, with plenty of helpful resources, it is an essential guide for would-be owners.

Carolyn Henderson is a journalist and author. She has written over twenty books on all aspects of horse care, her articles appear regularly in the *Times*, *Horse and Hound* and *Horse*, and she has wide experience of keeping, schooling and competing horses.

teach yourself | **dog training**
association of pet dog trainers

- Do you want a comprehensive guide to training your dog?
- Would you like your dog to be socially well-behaved?
- Do you need advice on all aspects of being a dog owner?

If you want your dog to be well-behaved then **Dog Training** is for you. Essential reading for all dog owners or those thinking of buying a dog for the first time, this book covers every aspect of kind, fair and effective dog training as well as authoritative advice on looking after your pet. Using positive, reward and motivational techniques, including clicker training, you will be able to train your dog to be obedient, sociable and, most importantly, to be a part of your family.

Association of Pet Dog Trainers offers pet dog owners a guarantee of quality when looking for dog training advice. The APDT abide by kind and fair principles of training and have written this book accordingly. For more information, visit www.apdt.co.uk

teach yourself	**keeping a rabbit** emma magnus

- Are you interested in keeping a rabbit?
- Do you know about the different breeds?
- Do you need guidance for care and behaviour?

If you have just bought, or are a hoping to own a rabbit, this book will prove indispensable. **Keeping a Rabbit** contains practical advice on breeds, equipment, maintenance, feeding and health for your pet, in addition to lots of helpful insights into behaviour and plenty of trouble-shooting tips. With information on breeding, exhibiting are even owning rarer breeds, this is all you'll ever need for a happy, healthy rabbit.

Emma Magnus is a qualified animal behaviour expert, consultant and journalist who specializes in small animals and who writes regularly for pet magazines and the media.

teach yourself	**keeping poultry** victoria roberts

- Do you want to know which breed lays best?
- Would you like advice on housing and equipment?
- Are you considering keeping ducks and geese?

Whether you want to start from scratch with a few hens, or branch into ducks, geese and other birds, **Keeping Poultry** is for you. It tells you which breed of bird lays best and gives useful guidance on housing, equipment and the necessities of day-to-day care. Covering all types of poultry, this guide offers advice on everything from exhibiting birds to meat production, with a full 'trouble-shooting' section and even tips for breeding your birds.

Victoria Roberts, BVSc MRCVS, is the author or editor of five books on keeping poultry, the Honorary Veterinary Surgeon for the Poultry Club, and the Editor of the Poultry Club newsletter.

teach yourself

how to win at horse racing
belinda levez

- Do you want to learn about different races and rules?
- Would you like advice on how to place a bet?
- Are you looking for help in selecting a winner?

How to Win at Horse Racing is designed both for newcomers to racing who want to understand the different types of race and bet, and for the more experienced punters keen to improve the odds of success. Fully updated with all the latest information on rules, grades and latest methods of betting, it is guaranteed to help you get the most out of your horse racing!

Belinda Levez is the author of a number of successful introductions to gambling, a former betting shop manager, and the editor of the online magazines *How to Win and Casinonet*.